*Praise for □* 

I was asked by a semin⸺ ⸺t way
to success?" My reply ⸺ ⸺y to success
is to replace bad habits ⸺ ⸺abits. If you are looking
for the good habits that will take you to success the fastest
way possible, *The Top 1%* by Dan Strutzel is the perfect book
for you."                              —Tom Ziglar, CEO of Ziglar Inc.

This extraordinary book cuts through all the ideas and
recommendations for success and gives you one powerful,
practical book full of proven strategies and techniques that
you can use immediately to start moving into the Top 1%.
                                             —Brian Tracy, author

An authentic role model and mentor, with the best advice
of the decade on getting to the very top and staying there.
Dan Strutzel has created a timeless and timely masterpiece!
                        —Denis Waitley, author, *Seeds of Greatness*

"Being in *The Top 1%* doesn't happen by accident and
though it eludes many, it is attainable by all. Dan has done
a remarkable job laying out a tried-and-true path to an
abundant life. As Dan points out, it starts with a decision.
If learning to make a committed decision is the only take-
away you receive from this wonderful book, I guarantee it
will be worth its weight in gold to you. Every success starts
with a decision!"

                —Bob Proctor, bestselling author of *You Were Born Rich*

"Due to the unprecedented changes happening in our economy that I explain in my new book, *The Sale of a Lifetime,* the people who will really thrive in the future will be those who strive to be in the Top 1% of their chosen profession. In this timely and thought-provoking new book, Dan gives you specific philosophies, strategies and techniques for ensuring that you are a part of this elite group of individuals."

—Harry S. Dent, Jr.

# *The* Top **1**%

## HABITS, ATTITUDES & STRATEGIES FOR EXCEPTIONAL SUCCESS

## DAN STRUTZEL

Published by Gildan Media LLC
aka G&D Media
www.GandDmedia.com

Front Cover image: Cindy Joy

Interior design by Meghan Day Healey of Story Horse, LLC.

Library of Congress Cataloging-in-Publication Data is available upon request

ISBN: 978-1-7225-1007-7

Manufactured in the United States of America by LSC Communications

10   9   8   7   6   5   4   3   2   1

*To my wife, Elvia,*
*my children—Kyra, Jeremy and Camden*
*and my parents—Lynne and Fred*
*who provided me the foundation of love*
*and wisdom that made this book possible.*

# Contents

# Introduction

As Founder and Chairman Emeritus of Famous Dave's of America, Inc. and as someone who has been blessed with great success on a professional and personal level, I am increasingly concerned about the criticism being leveled in our country at the Top 1%. Pitching this as a "battle" between the 1% and the 99% is not only counterproductive to our society but is terribly incorrect. The truth is that scores of entrepreneurs like myself, executives, salespeople, athletes, professionals including doctors and lawyers, and many others who have achieved high levels of financial success rarely think of themselves as being part of a group called "the 1%." One of the biggest misconceptions is that the 1% thrive on the misfortunes of the 99% which is an outrageous misunderstanding. Quite the contrary, most high performers are driven by the obsession to add tremendous value to their customers, constituents and share-holders. We live to create and give value—not to take. We spend every waking hour racking our brains as to how we can create something totally original that will make people happy—not at how we can "out-compete" others to success.

I overcame a childhood of limited means, poor grades, and a learning disability to achieve the American Dream—and I can assure you that my motivation did not come from joining an elite percentage of the population. My motivation came from finding out how to take something I love—namely great tasting barbecue—and make it accessible to millions of people worldwide. If I became a part of this "Top 1%", it happened only because of my desire to *serve* the 99%. My life story can be summed up this way, "I was able to take my backyard grill and turn it into a $500 million restaurant empire by learning and using the insights and tools you will hear about in this book."

That's what I love about this simple yet priceless book by my friend Dan Strutzel, *The Top 1%: Habits, Attitudes and Strategies for Exceptional Success*. This is not another book that perpetuates the great 1% versus 99% divide. It does not share unattainable gold-plated success stories by ogling the lifestyles of the elite, the rich and the famous. That is not a model of success I ascribe to, nor is it attractive to the vast majority of the Top 1% of income earners that I know. In this little gem, you'll discover why most of what you think you know about the Top 1% is a myth. You will become aware of the simple success truths that have eluded many of the 99% and that most people who achieve great success are motivated more by serving others, than by how many zeroes they have in their bank account. You will discover how everyone, regardless of their level of financial success today, can benefit from implementing the same habits as the Top 1%.

And here's the best of all. Dan will show you not only how to earn an income like the Top 1%, but also how to reach the Top 1% in the other vitally important areas of your life—from your friendships, to your family, to your community. In that spirit, Dan will show you that what is truly important in life is same whether your income is in the Top 1%, 5%, 50% or 90%.

Let me assure you that Dan is the perfect person to take you on this journey to the Top 1%. As a lifelong fan of personal development and achievement programs, I met Dan when he was the VP of Publishing at The Nightingale-Conant Corporation, one of top publishers of personal development wisdom in the world. He has published the leading authors and speakers in this sector, including Tony Robbins, Marianne Williamson, Brian Tracy and the late Sir John Templeton. During his 25 years with Nightingale-Conant he was exposed to the best ideas about success and personal fulfillment ever developed. I know firsthand that Dan is a profound thinker and dynamic speaker in his own right. When I asked him to speak at a charitable gala for my "LifeSkills Center for Business Leadership" he presented many of the ideas you'll read in this book. The packed house, ranging from recent grads to mid-career folks to aging Baby Boomers, was mesmerized, deeply touched and profoundly inspired. Once you are done with this book, you will see why.

We are living in uncertain times and many wonder if the American Dream is still possible. I believe it is *exactly* in these challenging times that the greatest opportunities are created. As Dan says, your journey begins with a simple decision. From my own humble beginnings to living the life I love, I can honestly say you'll never regret your decision to invest in this book.

Best of success,
"Famous" Dave Anderson
America's Rib King

# *The*
# Top 1%

# 1

# The Decision That Will Change Your Life

---◦●◦---

I'd like to invite you on a journey—one of the most significant and life-changing journeys you could ever take. It's a journey that most people dream of taking and a journey that others take pride in sitting out. But if I've done my job, at the end of this book I will have convinced you that the decision to take this journey marked a turning point in your life—for the better. It's the journey to the Top 1% of income earners and wealth producers in this country. And this road to the Top 1% isn't followed by just being a bit better or following the "traditional" rules of success. Following the familiar formulas for success will only get you to the top 20% of income earners.

No, to reach the Top 1%, you must take what the great poet Robert Frost called a "road less traveled." Because it is so lightly traveled, there are few maps or signposts in the broader culture to guide you on your journey. In this book, I'll draw out the map and identify the signposts very clearly for you, so you have all of the tools at your disposal not only to make the journey, but to arrive at your destination successfully.

While the Top 1% is most clearly identified by net worth or income, since these things are the easiest to measure, my goal in this book is far broader. We can all identify very wealthy individuals who are desperately unhappy and depressed, have left behind a string of broken relationships, and have no time to appreciate the fruits of their labor. Our goal is to get you into the Top 1% not only of income but of happiness and fulfillment, however you define that. For some of you, you'll want the time to travel. For others, you'll envision a life where you are happily married, and for some, a life where you have a positive impact as a parent. For others, you'll have charitable causes to which you'll want to dedicate a certain amount of your time and resources. Don't make the mistake of focusing all of your time and attention only on money and what money can buy, while neglecting the areas of your life that deliver the rich rewards that money *can't* buy.

Let's also keep in mind the best reason to make this journey. I'm indebted to the late personal development speaker and philosopher Jim Rohn for this key distinction. He said that the reason to set a goal of achieving a very aggressive and uncommon level of success is not just for the level of wealth, prestige, and influence that it will bring you, but rather what it will make of you to reach that goal. In order to achieve this level of success, you must not only get good at earning money—in fact we could say that this is actually a by-product. Rather, you must get good at a whole host of things, like self-discipline; commitment to a goal regardless of the roadblocks you encounter; an ability to deliver exceptional value to others; earning other people's trust; taking a long-term perspective; developing a high level of self-confidence; believing in your goals even when it seems that there are few others who share your vision; hanging out with high quality, positive people who want to make a difference in the world; and so much more. Truthfully, striving to join the Top 1% is probably the best thing you can do to ensure that you tap into the greatest level of your God-given potential while you are on this earth.

For those who ask: Why go through all of that effort, give up all of those easy weekends, or risk being laughed at or failing at your objective? Why give up that seemingly safe and secure job? Why would I want to join such a group that seems to receive such scorn from the media and our greater culture? Why? The best answer to that set of "Why?" questions is another set of questions: "Why not?" Why *not* spend the precious minutes of your one life on earth setting a goal that, regardless of whether you ever reach it, will make more of your potential than you could have ever dreamed? Why *not* be the person who has the opportunity to creative massive levels of value for millions of customers, thousands of employees, and most importantly, your loved ones? Why *not* take the next five years of your life to see how much you can earn, how much you can grow your skills, how much you can increase your confidence, how much you can increase your resilience, how much you can increase your productivity, and how much you can develop your ability to motivate and influence others? Remember, the next five years is going to pass either way—whether you decide to take the exceptional route, or the average route.

Here's a chilling fact: *today is the future destination of five years ago.* What do I mean? Simply this: Five years ago, you were probably thinking of what your life might be like in five years—which probably seemed so far off. *Today* is that future you dreamed about. How do you like your current destination? How could it be improved? How could it have been different if, five years ago, you had made the decision to join the Top 1%? I imagine that you could think of several areas of your life that could be improved by such a decision.

Well, here's the great news. You have another opportunity to make such a decision. The future you dream about five years from now will surely arrive—as swiftly as your present day has arrived. The only question is: Will you arrive at a destination that makes you proud? And will the process of getting to that destination have made you a stronger, happier, more charitable, healthier, and wealthier person?

Let me invite you right now, wherever you may be at this very moment, to make such a decision. Don't make it lightly or simply in passing as you blithely move on to other things. If you are driving, pull off the road. If you are working out, cooking, cleaning, doing outdoor work, or taking the dog for a walk—whatever you may be doing—please stop for a moment. Breathe deeply, and center yourself. Give serious and focused consideration to the decision you are about to make. The great personal development master Tony Robbins has said that a decision means to "cut off from any other possibility other than achieving the result." That's the kind of decision you are about to make. And, if you are ready, go ahead and make that kind of decision. If you had the interest in a book about how to join the Top 1%, I have no doubt you are ready to make that decision. So, no excuses. Go ahead and do it now.

Now that you have made the decision, take the rest of the day to celebrate and visualize what you will feel like in five years, having reached your goal of ascending to the Top 1% of wealth producers, income earners, and value contributors in the world today. Enjoy that vision. And get some good sleep tonight. Because tomorrow it's time to get to work. Tomorrow will be the first day of your five-year journey. And the ideas you learn here will be the tools you'll use to travel that journey successfully.

Before I begin to give you the tools—the ideas, techniques, and strategies to join the Top 1%, I want to tell you a bit more about myself and my qualifications to make such a bold claim. As you read Famous Dave Anderson's introduction, I'm sure you asked yourself more than a few times, "Who is this guy Dan Strutzel, and why should I trust him to teach me the essentials for joining the Top 1%?"

It's a fair question. The truth is that I'm not a person who's sitting on the mountaintop, having made the successful journey to the Top 1%, and telling you exactly what I did, so you can follow those same steps for your success. First, I don't believe in simplistic "x"-step formulas for something as important, complex, and ambitious as reaching the Top 1%. There are as many paths to achieving great success as there are human beings. But I do believe in principles and guidelines for success, and those can be studied, very much as the rules for a football game must be studied. Once those rules and guidelines are known, there are a million different ways to strategize to win a football game.

Second, I am a fellow traveler on this journey, just like you. As of this writing, I have not yet achieved this goal of reaching the Top 1%, but I am working hard to get there. And I'm following the exact ideas that I'll be sharing with you here. I am going to talk to you as a peer—traveling the journey together. This is the true meaning of "walking your talk." It is my hope that if we ever have the opportunity to meet or interact with one another, I will have earned that distinction.

My qualifications to teach you this material come from a career that spans over twenty-five years, working with hundreds of authors, business owners, and investors who are card-carrying members of the Top 1%. For many years, I was the vice president of publishing at the Nightingale-Conant Corporation, a world leader in personal and business development publishing for over fifty-five years. Currently I am the founder and CEO of Inspire Productions, assisting organizations and authors in the creation, production, and marketing of high-quality personal development content on multiple platforms that will inspire generations to come. I worked directly with some of the best-known authors in this arena, such as the late Zig Ziglar, Tony Robbins, Brian Tracy, Marianne Williamson, Jim Rohn,

Denis Waitley, Mark Victor Hansen, the late Wayne Dyer, and Byron Katie. In addition, I've worked closely with successful investing and wealth-building minds like Harry S. Dent Jr., Robert Kiyosaki, Sharon Lechter, Dolf de Roos, Mike Summey, David Bach, Ric Edelman, and John Cummuta. Additionally, I have worked closely with successful organizations that have used the principles I teach in their businesses—and have also spawned generations to achieve the Top 1%—organizations like Dale Carnegie Training, Ziglar Corporation, and the Napoleon Hill Foundation. The information I share comes not only from my own careful research and life experience, but also the collective wisdom of this incredible group of individuals and organizations who have blessed my life.

At the end of the day, the value I deliver to you here will come, more than anything else, from the results that the ideas you learn to produce in your own life. I see my role as your coach—assisting you in the creation and production of a high value life, and in the distribution of that value to hundreds, thousands, and even millions of others whom you will encounter on your journey. So let's get started.

# 2

# The Myths and Realities
# of the Top 1%

———◦•◦•◦———

The first step in our journey is to help you eliminate any
destructive beliefs you may have about joining the Top 1%.
Let's face a central truth head-on: For the last several years
in the United States there has been quite a public relations
campaign getting others to believe several myths about the
Top 1%. In order to do this, the media has created an arti-
ficial separation between the 1% and the 99%. They have
given the majority of the population a target, a focus for
all of the frustrations they may have about their lives, and
their perceived inability to succeed, at least at the level that
they would like. It seems that hardly a week goes by without someone reading an article, listening to an interview,
or watching a protest about how the Top 1% is destroy-
ing America, oppressing the 99%, rigging the economy to
serve only themselves.

As the great Earl Nightingale, the co-founder of the Nightingale-Conant Corporation, once said, "We become what we think about." And after a constant barrage against the Top 1% from the media, politicians, think tanks, and academics, many people have thoughts in their heads, even if they are very slight and subconscious, that being part of the Top 1% is somehow undesirable, and that achieving this goal will cause one to lose friends, to abandon one's values, or to be disliked. Nothing could be further from the truth.

There are several myths which have caused a great deal of confusion about the Top 1% and have served to cause people to think that its members are the source of just about every major problem in our culture (insert your favorite problem here). I'm going to identify five of the most prominent myths here, give you a detailed understanding of why each of them is flat-out wrong, and, in so doing, hopefully cause you either to change any negative beliefs you may have about the Top 1%, or, better yet, to give you more reasons to feel positively about your desire to join the Top 1%.

**Myth #1: The Top 1% is like a modern aristocracy: it is a fixed group of people who continue to earn high incomes for their lifetimes.**

This is probably one of the most common and unquestioned myths, because it fits people's desire to break things into simplistic black and white, either-or categories. It's easier for the media to frame an ideological war between the Top 1% and the 99%—if it's an "us versus them" kind of dichotomy and it's clear which group you belong to. But, like most things in life, the truth is much more complex. According to CNNMoney.com, it took an adjusted gross household income of $389,000 to be considered part of the Top 1% in 2011.

Statistics show that as of 2015, this household income amount has increased to about $400,000—far from the millions of dollars that most people would assume it takes to reach the Top 1%. But here's the startling fact pointed out by CNNMoney.com: "There are few lifetime memberships in the exclusive club of high-income taxpayers." In fact, there's a lot of turnover in the Top 1%. Membership can be fleeting, because many people are temporarily catapulted into the Top 1% or even top 0. 5% of tax filers by a windfall of some kind, such as proceeds from the sale of a business or from one-time capital gains.

In fact, nearly 60% of those in the Top 1% of taxpayers at the start of any ten-year period between 1987 and 2010 had dropped out by the tenth year. That's from a study by the U. S. Treasury Department. And the Tax Foundation found this: Of those who reported income of more than $1 million between 1999 and 2007, about half reported income that high for only one year.

Certainly income is very different from net worth and wealth, as some save and invest while others spend everything they make, or more, but the point remains. Many people who are considered part of the 99% will go in and out of the Top 1%, perhaps a couple of times, during their lifetimes. It is very difficult for one group to pin the focus of our cultural problems with income distribution and other related issues on this 1%—since that group will have many different members every single year. The truth is that the Top 1% is a fluid group with membrane-like borders, with people passing in and out. And thank God for that—since the goal of this program is to enable you to break into that group for as long as possible.

**Myth #2: The Top 1% are successful primarily because of luck, political connections, et cetera.**

This myth is probably the most pervasive, and also the easiest to believe—because it essentially absolves 99% of humanity from any sense of personal responsibility. It's comforting to believe, "If only I had gotten the same breaks, was born into the same family, had the same trust fund, was lucky enough to start a business at just the right time in the economy—on and on—then I too could have been just as successful."

There are a few important points to make here:

1. There is no doubt that luck plays a role in everyone's life—not just those of the Top 1%. We could say that we are all lucky to have met our spouse or significant other, lucky to have been born in the United States, lucky to be alive at all, given the incredible odds against it, and so forth. Yes, luck does play a role in everyone's life. The question here is whether luck is a *primary* influence.

2. Keep in mind that luck works both ways. Luck can play a role in increasing success, but it can play just as strong a role in increasing failure. For those who

are college football fans like me, you might recall the incredible finish to the Auburn-Alabama football game in 2014, when Alabama attempted a winning field goal on the final play of the game. The ball fell short and then was returned by Auburn for an improbable score with no time left on the clock to win the game. Was Auburn just lucky enough to be in the right place at the right time to win the game, or was Alabama unlucky enough not just to miss a field goal, but to miss it so badly that it fell right in the hands of the Auburn player? One person's luck is another person's misfortune.

3. Most importantly, luck is never the primary reason for a person's success, since luck cannot, of its own accord, deliver someone into the Top 1%. Luck, at best, gives a major assist to the well-prepared person who is in the arena, playing the game of life to win. It won't carry a person sitting on their couch, wasting their time away, to the corner office. And it won't multiply a single uninvested dollar. It will take that ambitious young employee with a great LinkedIn profile to the corner office when his superior decides to suddenly, or "luckily," leave the company. And it will take an invested dollar, multiplied beyond all expectation when it is invested, perhaps "luckily" in the right stock. In this sense, luck is never the primary cause of achieving success, since you must risk something, and must be working toward a well-defined goal, in order to activate it. It's been said that luck is when "preparedness meets opportunity." And, in

this case, it's the "preparedness" that is the primary factor in one's success—because it takes preparedness to notice and take advantage of the opportunity.

Dr. Richard Wiseman, author of *The Luck Factor,* said it another way: "Lucky people generate their own good fortune via four basic principles. They are skilled at creating and noticing chance opportunities, make lucky decisions by listening to their intuition, create self-fulfilling prophecies via positive expectations, and adopt a resilient attitude that transforms bad luck into good."

Notice how much of that definition lies within a person's control: being skilled, listening, creating, adopting a resilient attitude. These are all active terms suggesting that paradoxically, the only truly "lucky" successful people in the world are those who plan to be lucky.

**Myth #3: The vast majority of the Top 1% are born into privilege and have no conception of the struggles of the other 99%.**

This is a myth that certainly seems to be true, mostly because the vast majority of those we think are the Top 1% are people we see on TV or at the movie theater. They are the celebrities, movie stars, professional athletes, politicians, reality TV stars, and more. We think of such people as pampered multi-multi-millionaires who live in gated communities, drive Bugattis and Lamborghinis for hundreds of thousands of dollars, have personal trainers and plastic surgeons on call, and never set foot in a grocery store or wait in line for anything.

This view of the Top 1% is completely wrong. In fact, this caricature of the Top 1% is really only representative of the top 1% of the Top 1%. As Thomas Stanley, author of the mega best seller *The Millionaire Next Door,* taught us: the vast majority of wealthy and successful people in this country live in middle- to upper-middle-class neighborhoods, drive used or nonluxury American-made cars, and are "first generation wealthy"—in that they were not the beneficiaries of large trust funds or inheritances.

That said, there is one major area where the Top 1% is vastly different than the 99%—their spending and saving habits. In short, the Top 1% spend well below their means, spend vastly more of their money (than the 99%) on things that increase in value, and save an enormous amount—from 25% to 50%—of their income.

Here you can see that, for the most part, joining the Top 1% is a *choice.* It is a choice to delay one's gratification and make great sacrifices in one's lifestyle in the near term in order to gain the greatest amount of lifestyle freedom in the long-term. Or, as Jim Rohn used to say: "Do what you have to do as quick as you can, so you can do what you want to do as long as you can."

When you think about people in the Top 1%, you must realize that, for the vast majority of its members, reaching that milestone is the result of years of sacrifice and delayed gratification. In truth, for most of them, had they lived like the vast majority of the population, they could have lived an even greater lifestyle and had vastly more free time during their early years. That's because about 95% of our population spend beyond their means, charge more than they can afford on credit cards, buy or lease cars far more expensive than they can afford, and are anything but frugal. They buy that daily latte or two at Starbucks rather than making their coffee at home, for example. There are always the exceptions that keep this myth of privilege alive in our culture. They keep most people from realizing the uncomfortable truth: that if a majority of the 99% were to simply make the difficult choices to delay their gratification, live below their means, and employ the other ideas we've just discussed, they too could join the Top 1%.

**Myth #4: The Top 1% only serve to protect themselves and offer no value to the 99%.**

This is what I call the "politician's myth" about the Top 1%. It gets rolled out to the public by populists on both sides of the political spectrum at every election season. You know how this song goes: "All of the money and value being created in our economy goes directly to the Top 1%, and the rest of the hardworking people in the country—the 99%—get nothing." It's as if the Top 1% just serve to passively absorb all of the wealth in our country like a giant vacuum-sucking apparatus and wall themselves off in their wealthy communities, not caring at all about how the other 99% live.

This is not only an offensive and divisive characterization, it is also completely wrong. The truth of the matter is that in a free-market economy—and wherever you stand on government regulation, there is no doubt that the United States remains one of the strongest free-market economies in the world—the vast majority of people can only get rich while enriching others. Yes, of course, there are the outliers—the pornographers, scam artists, and black market drug dealers—but they are just that: outliers. The vast majority of the Top 1% in our economy can only get that way by delivering great value, value out of all proportion of their wealth, to the remaining 99%.

What's the proof of this? For one thing, we can compare standards of living today for the poor, middle class, and upper middle class, compared to thirty years ago. In the excellent book *The End of Prosperity,* authors Stephen Moore, Art Laffer, and Peter Tanous point out that "today most of the poor own things that once were considered luxuries, such as washing machines, clothes dryers, refrigerators, microwaves, color TV sets, air conditioning, stereos, cell phones, and at least one car. Amazingly, a larger percentage of poor families own these consumer items today than the *middle class* did in 1970." And can you imagine the typical middle-class teenager without access to a smartphone and a laptop for schoolwork and Netflix? Many of these products and services that are now provided at such low cost—from technological gadgets like computers and smartphones, to household appliances, to affordable "fast casual" dining options—have been developed by innovative entrepreneurs in the Top 1%. As Warren Buffett said just recently, "The babies being born today are the luckiest crop in history."

Buffett adds: "American GDP per capita is now about $56,000. As I mentioned last year, that—in real terms—is a staggering six times the amount in 1930, the year I was born, a leap far beyond the wildest dreams of my parents or their contemporaries. U. S. citizens are not intrinsically more intelligent today, nor do they work harder than did Americans in 1930. Rather, they work far more efficiently and thereby produce far more. This all-powerful trend is certain to continue: America's economic magic remains alive and well."

In short, value is being created for every American, regardless of class.

**Myth #5: The Top 1% are primarily full of passive investors who don't have to work for a living.**

This myth is pervasive throughout our society, from movies and books to our own creative imaginations about what it would be like to be well-off enough to be in the Top 1%. One imagines a person who has money stacked away in investments, earning them a rich passive income, as they spend time in yachts and swimming pools, golf courses, ski lodges, Gulfstream jets, and expensive restaurants.

Here's the reality: long work hours, times of punishing stress, lost sleep, and missed family occasions. According to Dalton Conley, chair of the Sociology Department at New York University: "It is now the rich who are the most stressed out and the most likely to be working the most. Perhaps for the first time since we've kept track of such things, higher income folks work more hours than lower wage earners do."

In addition, a study by economists Peter Kuhn and Fernando Lozano showed that since 1980, the number of men in the bottom fifth of the income scale who work long hours (defined as more than forty-nine hours per week) dropped by half. At the same time, long weeks for the top fifth of earners increased 80%. So, without a doubt, the vast majority of the 1% work for a living—they just work on different things and in a different way than the majority of the population.

We'll be revealing many of those key differences in this book. What's more, we'll also reveal several ideas on how to not only earn well, but live well, and give well. After all, what good is great success if it doesn't enrich your life and the lives of your family and your community? That's the vision of the Top 1% that we'll be sharing with you here.

Since we have just eliminated many of the myths that are the foundation of false beliefs that can hinder your desire to pursue that goal, it is time to give yourself some compelling reasons to increase your sense of urgency about reaching your goal. To return to my mentor, Jim Rohn, he would often say: "You can achieve just about any realistic goal that you set for yourself, if you have enough reasons." If you can make your reasons as strong and compelling as possible, you'll be astonished at how quickly you can turn your dreams into reality.

Let's end this chapter with a major action step: I want you to get out your laptop, your tablet computer, or even an old-fashioned yellow pad with pen or pencil, and write out five reasons why joining the Top 1% will make your life and the lives of those around you so much better. Again, make sure each of your reasons is as compelling, as descriptive, as emotional, and as specific as possible. It's your well-defined reasons, charged with emotion, that will pull you toward your goals faster than you ever thought possible. And if you're having trouble coming up with a compelling reason, read on. In the next chapter, I will introduce you to a universal reason why everyone should be motivated to become part of the Top 1%: *the fact that today, and even more so in the near future, the idea of a comfortable, "average" life is over.*

# 3

# Average is Over

The late Earl Nightingale, founder of the Nightingale-Conant Corporation, was one of the great personal development thinkers of our time. His program *Lead the Field* is one of the top-selling audio programs in history and has been nicknamed "The Program of Presidents" because of the number of former CEOs and presidents that owed a portion of their success to the ideas in that program.

As a former top executive at Nightingale-Conant, I had the pleasure of helping to publish and market many of Earl Nightingale's great ideas, and I still consider him to be a great inspiration and mentor. However, it's very interesting to go back after many years to some of the great classics, like *Lead the Field,* and reflect on what in those programs remains eternal and also on how much has changed in our twenty-first century world.

The general ideas of goal setting and achieving, developing a positive attitude, acting with integrity, striving for excellence, and managing one's time are timeless truths that will always have a place in anyone's personal development game plan. But quite often the way those ideas are expressed, and the assumptions that underlie those ideas, change radically as time moves forward. Of the great classics of modern personal development, *Lead the Field* dates back to the '40s, while *Think and Grow Rich* by Napoleon Hill was published in 1937, and *How to Win Friends and Influence People,* by Dale Carnegie, in 1936. And the latest updated edition of *Lead the Field* was published in the early '80s, just a couple of years before Earl Nightingale died.

Although the world of the '80s was very different from the '60s (in terms of social mores, the pace of change, et cetera), I think we can all agree that the changes we are experiencing in our present era dwarf the pace of change in any other period. While there is some debate about whether the level of significant innovation has accelerated, there is little debate that the impact of change is felt by a broader portion of the population more quickly than ever before. And these rapid changes, particularly technological changes, occur so fast that it is difficult to take stock of the impact they are having in our lives—both positively and negatively. It's important to step back once in a while—to take a 50,000-foot view of our lives—see how our adaptations to societal and technological changes are affecting us, and make conscious choices that will serve us to live the type of life that is in alignment with our values and goals.

My friend, Ken Blanchard author of *The One Minute Manager* and many other best-selling books, shared a quote with me many years ago, which he attributed to Albert Einstein. Einstein said: "Isn't it great that the telephone was invented, because I'll get to talk to my aunt who has moved to another town. But, then again, if the telephone hadn't been invented, maybe she wouldn't have moved." Here he was illustrating the vital point that with every technological change, there is both a gain and a loss. And it's important to take both the gains and losses into account when adopting new technologies, which is another way of saying new changes, in our lives.

With that in mind, I'm going to make the assertion in this book that there are certain success ideas, particularly for those who want to join the Top 1% that must be adapted to fit the modern times in which we live. Many of those traditional success ideas from those classic works are still true in their essence, but the ways in which they must be applied are different. And there are additional ideas that need to be considered because they reflect the very different society in which we live. In short, if these giants of success—Earl Nightingale, Napoleon Hill, and Dale Carnegie—were living today, how would they advise people on how to achieve exceptional success? That is what this book is all about.

I recently read a book that perfectly encapsulates the vastly different society and marketplace that we live in now. It is called *Average Is Over,* by Tyler Cowen, professor of economics at George Mason University. I'll make several book recommendations to you throughout this book, and this is the first on my list. If you haven't had the chance to read it, get a copy and read it as soon as you can. The book covers "Work and Wages in iWorld," "The Big Earners" (what we might call the Top 1%) and the professions that will be the "Big Losers" in this economy, and "The New World of Work" and how to succeed in it.

The main point is that in a globalized, mobile world, where automation is replacing jobs and career tracks no longer follow a straight line, the option of being average is over. High earners, including many of those in the Top 1%, according to Cowen, "are taking ever more advantage of machine intelligence and achieving better results. Meanwhile, every business sector relies less and less on manual labor, and that means a steady, secure life somewhere in the middle—average—is over."

Here is another vital quote from the book along these lines for our consideration:

> To put it bluntly, we are outsourcing some parts of our brain to mechanical devices and indeed we have been doing that for millennia, whether it be writing implements, books, the abacus, or a modern supercomputer. In response to all of these developments we have focused more on the skills the machines can't bring us.

There, in that last line, is the mission of this book on the Top 1%—to focus you on the habits, attitudes, and strategies for exceptional success that machines simply can't bring us. Machines can help us track our goals, manage our money, and even manage our health data, but they can't tell us what goals we should pursue or what our priorities should be; they can't offer our stamp of uniqueness, with our magical personality, and our sensitivity to the needs of our customers. And remember, by exceptional success I mean not just financial success, but success as a well-rounded human being.

In a technological world that serves to constantly distract us from what is truly important to our personal success, the ideas I'll be sharing with you are all the more timely. The success ideas that were presented in the classic programs of the past were created in an era when striving to be exceptional was a nice "option." Our post World War II economy was a perennially booming time for the middle class, the pace of life was steady, and incomes rose at their fastest rate for the broader population in our nation's history. One could live an average life and be very comfortable, with stable employment, an affordable lifestyle, and little concern about having one's job replaced by a machine or a worker abroad.

Those times are over. Today, in many ways, it's a far easier choice to commit to being exceptional—part of the Top 1%. To do otherwise is to subject yourself to a much more unstable, uncertain, and stressful life. And as I said earlier, even if you do not reach your goal, striving to do so will make you a more effective and fulfilled human being. So unlike the success books of the past, I encourage you not to look at these ideas as optional—look at the ideas that follow as *necessities*. It is only those things that are absolutely necessary in our lives that get done on schedule and are ultimately the only things that will change our lives for the better.

The information that follows is presented in several short chapters, so you can read them quickly and return to them again and again throughout your life. This is not an exhaustive list of every idea that you need to be successful, but rather a list of the things I feel I'm the most qualified to present to you with integrity and that I believe will be the most helpful to you.

Of course these ideas will not be exclusively my own. They are the distillation of the best ideas I've learned in the many years I have worked in the personal development industry. Like my friend Ken Blanchard, I like to think of myself as a "weaver"—a person who weaves all of the ideas he learns into a tapestry that works for him. I suggest that you adopt the same philosophy as you consider this incredible collection of ideas. No doubt you will like some better than others and find some more practical than others. But the real value you will get from this book is carefully weaving each idea, strand by strand, into your own unique tapestry. The goal is to make this book your own—to customize it to your specific set of goals and objectives.

And so we begin.

# 4

# The One True Joy

---

In preparation for this chapter, it was my goal to reflect on the many ideas I had learned over the years and see if there was one that stood out from all the others. "Was there a single idea," I asked myself, "upon which a successful life most depended? Without which one was almost assured to fail? Even further, was there one idea or principle that has made the most difference in my life, personally?"

As soon as I asked those questions in succession, the answer was clear. It is a principle that I have come to nickname "the one true joy"—and its name is *commitment*. Now before you reject this idea out of hand as clichéd or "obvious" I want you to look at this principle in a new way—with fresh eyes—as if you are learning it for the very first time. The reality is that commitment is the foundation upon which every successful life is built. But it is the least sexy, the least exciting and, quite possibly, the least appreciated success principle in the personal development lexicon. Yet, to return to my friend Ken Blanchard once again, the reason that he found most businesses failed was their failure to "keep their commitment to their commitment."

Now this seems like an oxymoron. Why would somebody need to keep a commitment to something they have already committed to? To understand what Ken means, we need to decipher between what I would call *cheap commitment* and *true commitment*. Cheap commitment is the sexy version of commitment—the kind that people make easily and quickly. "Sure, I'll call you back tomorrow." "This is the year that I'm going to get in shape." "Yeah, I can get you that report Wednesday, no problem." "Not now, I'm busy, son. I'll play catch with you tomorrow, I promise." These are the kind of commitments made on January 1 with great fervor, the kind that are used to pacify others or oneself with little thought or planning. They are cheap.

When I spoke of the one true joy, I was speaking about true commitments. Such commitments are made with great deliberation, determination, and motivation. When they are made, there is firmness in one's voice, a firmness that reflects the certainty of one's soul. This is not to say that a person making a true commitment has no fear or doubt. They often do. But their commitment itself is firm, is certain. There is no turning back.

The best analogy I can give you for the difference between the two is running a marathon. I have run over nineteen marathons over the past twenty-five years—from Seattle to Chicago to Boston. What I love about marathon running is that it is a goal the completion of which is completely "cheat proof." Except in rare cases, you simply cannot complete a 26.2-mile marathon without having made a true commitment. It involves months of training—running dozens of miles per week—with the payoff in some distant future. It involves reorienting one's diet, one's daily priorities, and most important, one's mental toughness. It is perfect true commitment training.

This is not to say that, when race day comes, everyone has made a true commitment. At the starting line, when the gun sounds, tens of thousands of runners confidently sprint off toward their destination. But experienced runners know that as many as 30% of those runners will never finish. Indeed the real race is won between miles eighteen and twenty-six— after the initial adrenaline rush has long passed and when the temptation to quit is almost unbearable. The only thing that keeps a runner going after mile eighteen is a true commitment to a goal made months, sometimes years, before.

Where is your mile eighteen? You may be at mile eighteen in your marriage, in your desire to bring your business into the black, in your aspirations for that big promotion, in your desire to build a stronger relationship with your teenage daughter. Mile eighteen comes along the path toward any worthwhile goal. My advice is to avoid the cheap commitments made at the starting line. Make the true commitment at mile eighteen to stay the course, all the way to the Top 1%. If you do, I promise you that the finish line will produce an emotion far deeper and more satisfying than that of happiness. It will leave you with a deep and everlasting feeling of joy.

# 5

# The Magical Attitude

I'd like to tell you about an extraordinary woman I know. By the age of eighty-six, here are just a few of the things she had taught herself to do: After talking to her landlord about several potholes that were a danger to the drivers in her apartment complex, and after waiting around for months for him to take action, she took matters into her own hands. She read up on the best type of cement mixture to fill a pothole, headed out to True Value Hardware, and filled the holes herself. Ten years later, those former potholes are still a distant memory. After receiving her first computer for Christmas six years ago, she put herself through a month-long, self-instructed tutorial on how to use a computer. She became more proficient with the services of her PC and the use of the Internet than your average twenty-one-year-old. She was up on all the Republican and Democratic presidential and congressional candidates for office and, over Thanksgiving dinner, could debate the pros and cons of each of their positions, leaving the rest of the extended family in stunned silence and awe, before the first slice of pumpkin pie was served! When any of her ten grandchildren were considering changing jobs, they always checked with her first because of her voracious appetite for reading newspapers and news magazines. She was as up-to-date on economic trends and hot industries as their peers! She still cooked from scratch, had long discussions over coffee with her close group of lady friends on a regular basis, e-mailed her elected officials about their "good" or "bad" decisions, and occasionally she even listened to the motivational programs I gave her!

OK, the cat is out of the bag. I'm talking about my grandmother. She just recently passed away at the ripe age of ninety-eight, and she was, to just about everyone who knew her, one of the strongest and most dynamic human beings that they had ever met. As for me, my grandmother is my hero—not just for how long she lived, but for *how* she lived.

We all intuitively know that our attitude about life has a great deal to do not only with the quality of our life experience, but with the quantity of our years—how long we will live. And recent research of centenarians—those people who live to a hundred years of age or longer—bears this out. Bradley Wilcox, Craig Wilcox, and Makoto Suzuki, in their best-selling book *The Okinawa Program,* did an in-depth study of the lifestyle habits of Okinawan people, who, on average, live many years longer than the average person in an industrialized country. While they did discuss some unique dietary and exercise factors that may have a slight effect on their longevity, by far the greatest factors were attitudinal in nature. In particular, their attitudes could be described with the following characteristics: an engagement with life, an open mind, and a willingness to learn new things. In the case of the Okinawan people, many of these attitudinal, dietary, and exercise factors are cultural in nature. Everyone tends to live the same way.

Unfortunately, these factors are not inherent in our culture here in the West. In fact, for a first-world, industrialized country, our overall health, and the health of our attitudes in particular, leave a great deal to be desired. Why is this? We live in the richest country known to man. We have the World Wide Web, libraries, with educational institutions at our fingertips. We are free to work where we choose, live where we choose, and believe what we choose. More than any other people living at any other time in history, we have it made. Yet statistics show that the average person in this country reads less than one full book per year. Many cultural commentators like Charles Sykes, author of *A Nation of Victims,* and business leaders like Dan Sullivan, founder of The Strategic Coach program for entrepreneurs, lament the sense of entitlement that seems to grip many people in our nation. In fact Dan Sullivan has given it a label: "the entitlement attitude." Contrary to the attitudes of my grandmother and the Okinawan people described above, this cancerous attitude says, "I am owed something from society." To go even further, the entitlement attitude often says, "I am owed something from society, regardless of how much or how little I give back to society." Partly as a result of this cancerous attitude, we have some of the lowest educational achievements, highest crime rates, and poorest health scores of any first-world, industrialized country.

One of the most important initial steps that every person who wants to join the Top 1% of the most successful and fulfilled people in the world must take is to eradicate the entitlement attitude from their lives, and to adopt what I call the *Magical Attitude*.

It's the same attitude that those who want to live not only a long life, but a high-quality life, practice every day. *This Magical Attitude is the attitude of lifelong learning.* This attitude encompasses all of the qualities we talked about before—an engagement with life, an open mind, and a willingness to learn new things. It's an attitude that says, "If I need something in my life, society doesn't owe it to me. It is up to me to take advantage of the incredible resources at my fingertips and to educate myself on how to get what I need." It is the attitude that drives someone to fill potholes and proactively write their congressman at eighty-six years of age. It is the attitude that, when life slows you down, forces you to get hip replacements; rather than cursing the world and withdrawing into a life of cynicism and regrets, you join an exercise class. It is the attitude that works with, rather than against, the law of cause and effect. And, when adopted, it is the attitude that, like magic, will turn every obstacle in your life into an opportunity.

# 6

# Become a Prime Mover

There has probably been no more controversial, and yet influential, novelist during the twentieth century than Ayn Rand. Her classic novel *Atlas Shrugged* has competed with Dale Carnegie's *How to Win Friends and Influence People* for years as the second all-time bestselling book next to the Bible. Nearly every high school or college student has read one of her works as part of their core curriculum. And her ideas have shaped the thinking of many of the country's most successful CEOs.

While I have many areas of profound disagreement with Ayn Rand—for example, her rejection of altruism and spirituality and her tendency to oversimplify complex life issues into simplistic objective maxims—she does have one concept that has made a great impact on me, the truth of which has only become more evident as I have spent more years in the marketplace. This is her concept of the Heroic Man and Woman, or what she has called the *prime mover*. Ayn Rand's novels are filled with examples of such heroic individuals, who contribute vastly more value to society than the average person, and whose leadership and ingenuity are essential to keeping the engine of an organization working. In fact, in the conclusion to *Atlas Shrugged,* all of the Heroic Men and Women go on strike and, as a result, the society grinds to a halt.

One of the most familiar phrases heard in the workplace during the early 2000s and now in the mid-2010s is, "no one is indispensable." In fact, if you ask a person on the street whether or not they could be subject to a sudden layoff, you'll often hear the phrase repeated almost reflexively, "Well, I think I work hard and I hope I'm safe. But, as you know, no one is indispensable." I disagree with this idea. While skills can certainly be replaced—manufacturing, accounting, negotiating, selling, et cetera—there are certain human beings that bring such uniqueness in their performance of these skills that they simply can't be replaced.

I'm sure you can think of individuals whose departure had an enormous effect on the performance of an organization. What happened to the win-loss record of the Chicago Bulls when Michael Jordan and Phil Jackson departed in the late 1990s? What happened to the stock price of General Electric when CEO Jack Welch retired? How did each of Jerry Seinfeld's co-stars fare in their own TV series, post-*Seinfeld*? How did Starbucks stock and in store performance hold up when their founder and CEO, Howard

Schultz, decided to reduce his involvement in the business several years ago?

In each case, I assert that there was, indeed, an indispensable individual, a prime mover, whose contributions were more than the sum of their skills and raw talent. It was this individual's uniqueness and his or her ability to get things done that transcended all others. And these indispensable individuals are, almost without exception, members of the Top 1%.

Now I'm sure you're thinking, "But these are larger-than-life examples—truly the exceptions. How can I, a middle manager at a small manufacturing company, truly make myself indispensable to my organization?" This is a valid point. However, I do not believe that a person has to be the CEO of a corporation or the star basketball player—in other words, "heroic" in the grand sense of that term—to be considered indispensable. Indeed, there are many companies and other types of organizations where individuals at all levels have acted as prime movers.

I remember a story that one of my favorite people and authors, Barry Farber, author of *State of the Art Selling* and *Diamond in the Rough,* told me about a bellhop named Smitty at the Marriott Marquis Hotel in Atlanta. Smitty was renowned for his extraordinary service, incredible can-do attitude, and infectious smile. He remembered everyone by name—remembered their favorite rooms, their favorite room service items, and even the names of their wives and children. He had become so renowned that baseball players, politicians, and other celebrities actually requested him for their service needs prior to arriving to the hotel. He was so legendary and beloved that these high-profile individuals wouldn't even think of staying anywhere but the Marquis when coming to Atlanta. It could be argued that Smitty was as essential to the ongoing success of the Atlanta Marriott Marquis as any of its employees.

So whether you're the CEO or a mid-level or entry level employee, here are a few steps you can take to make yourself indispensable to your organization:

1. **Spread yourself thin.** Some career manuals are preaching that you should only "build your own brand" and look out for number one, selecting only those projects that are good résumé builders. This might be a good strategy for someone whose career strategy is a lifetime of job-hopping, but if you are looking to grow with your current organization and make yourself indispensable, this strategy is incomplete. I say you also need to "spread yourself thin" by finding ways to become extraordinarily valuable to several different areas of your organization. Make sure that the key people of every department know you well and regard you as an extremely helpful individual. Become known as someone who takes the time to service all departments and individuals, not just those projects that are important to your boss. If you get a reputation as a self-serving individual and your boss leaves or is let go, your path out the door is imminent.

2. **Give it your stamp of authenticity.** What qualities do you have that are unique to your personality? These are the qualities that everyone, from family members to co-workers, comment on again and again. It may be an incredibly positive attitude, an attention to detail, a flair for eccentricity, being a great people person, et cetera. Find a way to infuse that quality in every task you undertake in your organization. Skills can be easily replaced; authentic individuals performing those skills in unique ways cannot.

3. **Become truly excellent at what you do.** There is no substitute for excellence—especially for those who seek to become part of the Top 1%. You can be authentic and helpful, but if you don't produce results, your time in any organization will be limited. Identify the three key skills that are central to producing bottom-line results for your company. Create your own self-directed university around these three skills and begin to tackle each skill, one at a time, in three-month increments. Do this by taking seminars on this skill, listening to audio programs on this skill, finding a mentor to coach you on it, et cetera. Nine months from now, you should graduate from your self-designed university with an A+ in results and a bulletproof career.

4. **Follow up immediately.** In a twenty-four-hour economy, where the 200 e-mail and ten phone mail day is no longer uncommon, people have become more accustomed to long delays in receiving

responses to their messages. You can use this to your advantage to help stand out from the crowd. Develop the reputation of someone who follows up immediately. Use the advice of my friend, David Allen, productivity expert and author of the classic book on productivity *Getting Things Done*. He has developed the "two minute rule" for responding to messages. He says to ask yourself with every e-mail or voice mail, can I respond to this in two minutes or less? If so, respond to it now, because it will take you longer to file it or reconsider it than respond. Follow this one rule, and it will label you as a lightning-quick responder on nearly 90% of your messages, and you'll form a powerful impression of someone who is committed to and in charge of your work.

5. **Always have a "wow" project.** We all have projects that are typical and expected, that fit neatly within our job descriptions. To stand out and make yourself indispensable, you need to create at least one unique project, outside the box of your current job description, that helps your company innovate and grow in new directions. It's the kind of project that solves a major problem for your company, builds your reputation as a proactive contributor, and elicits a "wow" from your superiors and co-workers. Perhaps it's coming up with new packaging for your product that is both more attractive and cost effective. Perhaps it's putting together a public relations task force inside your company to

get the word out on your product line. Perhaps it's helping to develop a new intranet inventory management system.

Do these things and you'll become one of the prime movers in your organization—an indispensable person that keeps the engine of results in high gear. And you'll have taken a vital step in becoming part of the Top 1%.

# 7

# The Art of Discipline

HOW THE TOP 1% GET THEMSELVES
TO DO WHAT THE 99% WON'T DO

William Feather, author of *The Business of Life,* once said: "If we don't discipline ourselves, the world will do it for us."

That statement, uttered many years ago, is even more relevant today. I like to compare the topic of discipline to that of a basketball player practicing free throws. Any basketball player will tell you that the monotonous process of shooting free throws over and over, sometimes dozens a day, is one of their least favorite exercises in preparing for a game. Yet the fundamental skill of hitting your free throws, especially when the game is on the line, is the difference between an average or good basketball player and a champion.

Likewise, while everyone would acknowledge that discipline is a fundamental building block of a successful life, I can tell you, as the president of Inspire Productions, who continually researches and develops content for the most popular topics on personal development and skill building, that few people want to discuss, let alone study, the topic of discipline. Why is this? Perhaps it lies in the definition of discipline itself. The best definition of discipline I've ever heard is *the ability to delay gratification to honor a higher principle or value.* Thus the definition of discipline itself acknowledges the necessity of postponing what we want in the short term for a greater longterm benefit. And the truth is, very few people are willing to postpone anything—even watching their favorite nightly television show—for a long-term goal somewhere out there in the distant future. For most people, as personal development speaker Jim Rohn says, "are unwilling to pay the price since the promise isn't clear."

Yet, to return to the quote from William Feather, the reality is that discipline is inevitable—either we discipline ourselves to achieve our own self-chosen goals and ideals, or the world will shape us toward its goals and ideals— goals and ideals that may have nothing to do with our own sense of purpose, happiness, and fulfillment.

This truth applies to every aspect of our lives. In the workplace, disciplined people *control* their day so they work on results-producing activities that contribute the most value to their businesses or organizations, while undisciplined people *are controlled* by their days—responding to a never-ending, ceaseless array of urgencies, whether they contribute to their overall productivity or not. As parents, disciplined people resist the tendency to respond to their children on impulse. Instead they choose a response, based on their self-chosen values, that will most contribute to the child's long-term wellbeing. Undisciplined people are chaotic in their response to their children's demands, responding purely on impulse, with little regard to what is best for the child's character. As spouses, disciplined people take the time to build the foundation of their relationship every day—by doing little things like writing notes to their spouse, planning nights out together, and avoiding retaliation for their spouse's moodiness. Undisciplined people, on the other hand, are often so overwhelmed that they are narcissistic in their response to their spouses, asserting only their own needs and being unwilling or too exhausted to take their spouse's perspective.

Notice that the continual theme running throughout these examples is just as William Feather suggested. Disciplined people follow their own self-chosen values and choose actions and responses based on those values. Undisciplined people follow the whims of the world's demands, and thus are never in control and are constantly reacting to stimuli imposed by others. The failure to discipline oneself on a consistent basis is the difference between being average and being in the Top 1%.

Now please understand, the above examples are ideals. Every one of us is likely to be disciplined at some things and undisciplined at others, and I don't want to suggest that anyone can be perfect in every major area of life. However, I have a few suggestions that I believe will help you to look at discipline not as a chore, but as an exciting challenge.

First, rather than looking at discipline as a long-term, laborious effort, look at it as *the daily process of controlling your choices in every area of your life.* Stephen Covey, in his fabulous book, *The Seven Habits of Highly Effective People,* states that what defines us as human beings is our ability to choose our response to any stimuli. Animals have no choice—they encounter a stimulus and react. Humans, on the other hand, encounter a stimulus and can use their minds to choose the most effective response.

This skill is required more than ever before in our history. In our global, interconnected economy—where computer processing power doubles every eighteen months—we are being bombarded with what some analysts have called "the tyranny of choices." By "tyranny" they mean a never-ending barrage of information that demands our decisions and responses.

But make no mistake. This is not a tyranny—it is your greatest ability and challenge. The key in this economy is not to abandon choices and surrender to the push and pull of circumstances, but to gain the ability to choose what to focus on and what to ignore. Don't abandon your ability to choose. So the next time your boss gives you an urgent project, you catch your child in a lie, or your spouse screams at you for being late, how will you respond? The choice is yours.

But you might say, "How to do I know which things to focus on and which things to ignore? My life is so hectic, I'm so busy, how can I ensure that I'll make the right choices in the heat of the moment?" This is a common concern, and in many ways, a very modern one. In today's fast-paced world, the common response that you almost always hear when you ask how someone is doing is, "I'm so busy." But this response is, in many ways, a reflection of the problem we have been discussing. Being busy, if it is a deliberate conscious choice, is often fine. But for most people, being busy and stressed-out is often a reflection of an undisciplined life, where the world is in control instead of oneself.

*Therefore the next step is to consciously create a list of your top five values in life.* Or if you find this exercise difficult, you could begin by constructing a mission statement for your life. Once you have done this, put the list on several index cards, say five, and put them in places that you visit often throughout the day. One could go in your bathroom, one in your car, one on your nightstand, one on your desk at work, et cetera. When you see these often, they will begin to form an imprint on your brain, a screening device, in essence, that will prevent you from making choices that are not in alignment with your values. Someone once said that if you have a larger YES burning inside of you, it's easy to say NO to the little things. Make your values your YES, and the discipline to say NO to the little things will become easy.

Finally, and most importantly, *learn to love the plateau*! Now what do I mean by that? Philosopher George Leonard introduced this concept many years ago in his book *Mastery* and it is one of the most powerful I have ever heard for disciplining yourself to stay the course with a "right action." Leonard says many people assume that disciplining yourself to do anything—in Leonard's case, to become a black belt in tae kwan do—should lead to continual and gradual improvement until you have reached your goal. In reality, Leonard says that most growth occurs in sudden bursts, with long stretches in between of what seems like no improvement—the plateau. He adds that most people abandon a course of discipline because they become addicted to the sudden bursts of growth and become discouraged when these do not happen quickly. The key to growth is learning to love the plateau, knowing that the next sudden burst of growth may occur at any moment.

So take control of your choices, know and commit to your values, and learn to love the plateau. Those essentials are vital to getting to and remaining in the Top 1%, and they are the ingredients to a marvelous recipe I call "a life worth living."

# 8

# The Willingness to Be Terrified

HOW THE TOP 1% HANDLE FEAR (PART ONE)

The scene was a sold-out conference of over 700 speakers and trainers in sunny Los Angeles called Mark Victor Hansen's Mega Speaking University. Mark Victor Hansen is the co-author of the best-selling *Chicken Soup for the Soul* series, with over 80 million copies in print worldwide. I was asked by Mark to join his panel of speakers for the event, giving a presentation titled "How to Create Your Nightingale-Conant Best Seller." This was back in 2005, and while I had done a fair amount of public speaking in college, and had worked with public speakers for over twelve years as a publishing executive, I was far from what you would call a professional speaker.

Of course I was honored and humbled to be part of Mark's exclusive panel of professional speakers, presenting to an audience of professional speakers. OK, I must come clean: I was honored, humbled, and *terrified*! Speaking at a small group event at my church or behind a microphone at my company was one thing, but speaking to a huge group of people who knew every trick of the trade—that was quite another. And that wasn't all. When I arrived at the event and was escorted to the ballroom, I was shocked to see two huge projection screens on each side of the stage, complete with professional lighting and rock music. This wasn't just a speaking event, it was an entertainment extravaganza!

While a part of me was excited beyond words, another part of me wanted to sneak back out of that auditorium, gather my bags, check out of that hotel, and catch the next plane back to Chicago. I thought: *What if I forget my speech? What if my PowerPoint presentation doesn't work? Do they really care what I've got to say?* These thoughts clouded my consciousness as Mark Victor Hansen was announced. The music blared, the lights flashed, and the crowd roared. Here was Mark Victor Hansen, one of the greatest speakers on the planet—and I had to follow this act? I was scheduled to speak the next day.

The next day arrived. I had practiced my speech over a dozen times as I paced back and forth in my hotel room. My mind raced with random thoughts of doom: *I don't have enough jokes. Mark told a lot of jokes. I've got to put in more jokes. I've got too many details. I need more inspirational stories. My PowerPoint is too simple. I've got to give it more pizzazz.* My heart pounded faster than a Phil Collins drum solo. Two hours and counting. Not enough time to change anything. Was everything OK?

Then, suddenly and without warning, I was hit by an awareness of calm and peace. I had done everything possible to prepare for this event. I had put everything I knew about producing incredible audio experiences into a one hour presentation; I had held nothing back. I had done my very best to prepare. Then I heard God whisper in His ever-so-subtle way: "Dan, you're a lot better at being you than somebody else. Give this presentation as best you know how, but do it with integrity. Go get 'em!" My heart came back into my chest. I decided to leave all of my forced jokes out. I put in a few stories, but kept the details. This is what the audience wanted of me—details on how to make an incredible audio experience. Anything less would be cheating them.

As I sat in the metaphorical green room behind the stage, waiting for my name to be announced, the calm somehow stayed with me. I was minutes from being ushered on stage, a microphone attached from my ear, and 700 guests waiting just beyond the curtain, yet somehow I was calmer and more focused than I was after arriving that first day. My name was called, the music went up, and I jumped out on stage. Suddenly my mouth went on autopilot, and I delivered my speech just the way I'd planned it. Oh sure, I had a few cold sweats and "pinch me" moments, but as I focused on delivering value to an audience I so admired, I felt what scores of other public presenters have felt before: a confidence unmatched.

Quite often, much like self-esteem, we assume that confidence is something that can be acquired through repeated affirmations, visualizations, and "attitude adjustments."

While all of these techniques do have their place, there is no substitute for *doing*. Think of all of these techniques like the helium in a balloon, while the *doing* of the activity itself is like the clamp on the opening of the balloon. Affirmations, visualizations, and attitude can puff you up and take you higher, but only if you put on the clamp of real activity again and again. Otherwise all of that helium will escape nearly as fast as you put it in, leaving no lasting effect.

Similarly, recent research has indicated that self esteem is most affected by two things: real achievements and what psychologists call *basic trust*. While basic trust is something established between parents and children at the very early bonding stage, we can all effect real achievements in our lives. And "real achievements" is another term for "doing" an activity. Indeed in this sense an achievement does not even mean that we have been successful. It means achieving an outcome and doing the thing that we fear most.

In many ways, I believe that my confidence to stand up at Mark's mega-event was not established through affirming my way to confidence as I jumped on stage. It was established from my *willingness to be terrified*. To give you a better idea of what I mean, think back to the first time you jumped into a pool when you were learning how to swim. Or think back to your first date. Wouldn't you agree that the act itself was far less taxing than the restless anxiety that preceded the event? So couldn't it also be said that the willingness to live with that anxiety and move through it was the most important step in establishing your confidence, whether in learning how to swim or in dazzling the opposite sex?

Oliver Wendell Holmes has a great quote about simplicity that applies here. He said: "I would not give a fig for the simplicity *this* side of complexity; but I would give my life for the simplicity on the *other* side of complexity." Likewise I have learned that the confidence that precedes anxiety, terror, and any other uncomfortable emotion pales in comparison to the confidence on the other side, because the confidence on the other side is real. It is born of a real struggle, a real action, a real achievement. It is the kind of confidence that leaves you fully satisfied. And it is the kind of confidence that doesn't leave your balloon, or your spirit, deflated.

If you hope to join the Top 1%, you have to be exceptional. And the path to being exceptional is uncommon and requires a willingness to endure prudent risks and stretch beyond your comfort zone—stretching all the way to the other side of complexity. If you don't feel this sense of disorientation and discomfort once in a while, it's very likely that you are not challenging yourself enough—and are not pushing yourself to new heights. Remember, average is over.

So the next time you're about to take on a challenge that leaves you a bit terrified at the thought of it, don't let it stop you. Say to yourself, "Aha, here it is. Here's the gateway to greatness." Then jump out on stage. The best is yet to come.

# 9

# Let Your Fears Polish You

In this chapter, we're going to focus on perhaps the most central issue to humankind since the dawn of the new millennium: *conquering fear*. For us as a culture, the '90s were considered to be a modern Golden Age—with the stock market roaring to new highs daily, employment at an all-time high, a surplus in the government back account, the dawn of a revolutionary new form of technology (the Internet), and, for the most part, especially during the second half of the '90s, one of the most peaceful periods in modern history.

How things have changed. Since the tragic events of 9/11, we have moved from the new economy and the Golden Age to the post-bubble economy and now, in the mid-2010s, what we might call the Age of Terrorism. The wide-eyed adolescent hope of the '90s has matured into a middle-aged sense of realism, if not outright skepticism. Culturally, we seemed to be locked in a permanent state of orange alert—fearing to take bold steps into the future because we don't want to be caught off guard by the next terror attack.

Such terror attacks are not only cultural, they are personal. Every time we strive to take a major growth step in our lives, outside of our comfort zone, fear seems to resist our attempts to move forward. A speech to your new executive team, competing in your first marathon, walking down the aisle to make a lifelong commitment to a future spouse, or delivering your first child—all are events that are greeted with the paradoxical twin emotions of excitement and perhaps incomprehensible fear.

Although learning to conquer fear is not new for us as individuals, it is quite new for us as a culture. Truthfully, there has probably never been a greater time in history, other than the Great Depression, where people felt that they were more justified to bury their head in the sand and just "survive." And yet there has likely never been a greater time in history where conquering fear was more necessary. It is both the answer to our problems and the antidote to future problems, individually and culturally. People in the Top 1% of our society are not spending their time living in fear—they are spending their time finding solutions and focusing on areas that they can control. This brings to mind the essence of the Serenity Prayer: "God grant me the serenity to accept the things I cannot change, the courage to change the things I can, and the wisdom to know the difference."

What is some good, practical advice for conquering fear that will enable a person to live a life that the influential Jesuit priest John Powell called, "a fully human, fully alive" way of life—living fully extended, with hopeful abandon, in pursuit of your most important goals?

In doing some research on this topic, I came across several common quotes that served to define the nature of fear, and gave prescriptions for eliminating it. Try a few of these on for size:

*FEAR: False Evidence Appearing Real.* —UNKNOWN

*He who fears something gives it power over him.*
—MOORISH PROVERB

*Keep your fears to yourself, share your courage with others.*
—ROBERT LOUIS STEVENSON

*Nothing in the affairs of men is worthy of great anxiety.*
—PLATO

This first group of quotes embodies what I would call the "fear is the enemy" philosophy. Each suggests that fear is either something unreal or something to be completely avoided—something unnecessary. But then I came across another series of quotes on fear. Try these on for size:

*Anything I've ever done that ultimately was worthwhile, initially scared me to death.* —BETTY BENDER

*To fear is one thing, to let fear grab you by the tail and swing you around is another.* —KATHERINE PATERSON

*Do the thing you fear and keep on doing it . . . that's the quickest and surest way ever yet discovered to conquer fear.*
—DALE CARNEGIE

*The conquest of fear lies in the moment of its acceptance.*
—UNKNOWN

This second group of quotes embodies what I call the "fear as friend" philosophy. Each of these suggests that fear is not necessarily something to be avoided, but something that, within limits, informs and instructs.

I must admit that earlier in my life, I subscribed to the "fear as enemy" philosophy. I tried either to think, visualize, or explain away my fears as illusions or to force them out of my consciousness by sheer will—treating them like a poison that, if left unattended, would sabotage any possible chance I had for success at any venture—be it in my career or personal life.

In one instance I was preparing to meet the parents of a girlfriend who lived in Des Moines, Iowa. As I made the car trip up from my hometown of Chicago, I remember squelching my fear by refusing to allow any fearful thoughts into my consciousness. I spent my seven-hour car trip visualizing exactly how I wanted the meeting to go and not allowing myself to think of any uncomfortable silences, looks of disgust, or embarrassing moments.

While the meeting went fine, I can remember how obsessed I became with my own thoughts and the impression I was making on them throughout the entire visit. Truthfully, I was so obsessed with squelching my fear that I ended up having no available energy for living and experiencing what was really happening moment by moment. I also robbed myself of the education that harboring my fears would have given me—reflecting on where they were coming from. Why was I so concerned about someone not liking me? Why did I feel like I needed to prepare, rather than just presenting myself as is, warts and all?

Over the years, my approach to fear has clearly shifted to the second camp—"fear as friend." I particularly resonate with the quote "The conquest of fear lies in the moment of its acceptance." Once you are able to name your fear, and to live with it, you are well on the way to conquering its negative effects over you.

You see, when we talk of conquering fear, we don't want to conquer its ability to instruct and inform our lives. The only thing we want to conquer is its ability to immobilize us—to prevent our growth. Yet, paradoxically, this is even more likely to happen when we refuse to acknowledge its existence. The popular self-help author John Bradshaw has illustrated this idea with great clarity in his brilliant work on addictions. According to Bradshaw, the denial of our true self and our true emotions, including our fears, through any available technique does not make them go away. Rather, Bradshaw says, "they become like a hungry dog in the basement," continuing to fester away until one day the dog bursts through the basement door with unforeseen rage.

This is why I have found that the first quote I shared, that "FEAR" is "False Evidence Appearing Real," although used by many self-help authors, represents a misleading and flawed philosophy. Even if what we fear never comes to pass, to us the feeling of fear is still real. We can feel it in the pit of our stomach, in our racing heartbeat and sweaty palms—and we need to learn why it is there and what it can teach us. In short, we need to let our fears polish us.

What do I mean by letting our fears polish us? Think of a beautiful BMW luxury classic car model that an owner has had for over thirty years. While it still runs beautifully, its exterior has been scratched through the years, and its black color has dulled into a listless, dusty gray. Now imagine you take that BMW to a car detailing center. They clean the car's interior and exterior, touch up the scratches with new paint, and finish it off with a polish that makes the car shine and sparkle like new. When the car comes out of the detailing center, it is as impressive as a brand-new BMW. Because it retains its character as a classic BMW model no longer in production, it has been preserved with the quality of a brand-new car.

In many ways, the car becomes more impressive, more valuable to its owner, than a new car driven off the lot. In a similar way, we have no doubt been dinged and dulled by negative experiences in our lives, which have caused fears to bubble up from our subconscious. If we allow our fears to control us, or if we push them under the rug, we begin to rust—like a classic car that has failed to be preserved. But the process of accepting our fears and courageously working through them is like a polish that preserves and refines us—leaving us with a lasting, classic shine. It's not the shine of an enthusiastic youngster who has never been through the bumps and bruises of life (or of a new car that has never been driven off the lot), but the shine of a mature adult who has faced his or her fears head-on, and emerged with a sense of wisdom and self knowledge that is evident to all.

So if you're currently struggling with a fear that is holding you back, let me offer you six suggestions—not for avoiding it—but for letting it inform and instruct you.

1. **Let your fears gently pass through you.** Think of your fears like running water washing over your hands. Look at them long enough to identify them, to note them, but let them pass—do not put up a dam. If you refuse to attach negative emotions to them and just watch them pass, you'll gain great self-knowledge without being immobilized. Try this when you're giving your next public presentation. Feel the fear emerge from within you, note it, even laugh at it, and then imagine it passing through and beyond you. Then give the speech without any attachment to it. Before long, your fears will cease to have control over you.

2. **Treat fears as your life school, your curriculum.** Every time fears emerge, imagine that they are your own self-designed (or more appropriately, soul-designed) university—they are your curriculum to be mastered. You only pass the test when you do the work of achieving whatever goal is on the other side of that fear. So if you're afraid of the water, the deep end of the swimming pool is your goal. And the final exam is plunging into the water and swimming to the other side. Thinking of your fears as your self designed school or university turns your fears into an objective project rather than a subjective nightmare.

3. **Stop. Act. Think.** While we should learn from
   our fears, that doesn't mean we should give them
   more time and attention than they deserve. Many
   of us stew over our fears for hours, days, months,
   or, God forbid, years, before we act to master them,
   if we ever do. If you've been immobilized by a fear
   for some time, the only way to master it is to catch
   yourself stewing over the fear. Then *stop* yourself by
   making a physical gesture, perhaps a clap, a slap in
   the face, a shake of the head. Act immediately and
   do the thing you fear, and allow your thinking to be
   done after you've completed or are in the midst of
   your feared action.

I tried this technique several years ago when my family
and I moved into an established neighborhood in the sub-
urbs of Chicago. A few weeks after we moved in, we had
met very few of our neighbors. They all had established
groups of friendships developed over the years, and were
not eager to reach out to the new couple on the block. I
remember seeing about eight of our neighbors on the front
porch of a house across the street from ours, sipping mar-
garitas and laughing their hearts out, as I was out in our
backyard mowing the lawn. While I desperately wanted to
meet them, fear welled up inside of me with thoughts like
*they wouldn't want to meet you, they already have a group
of friends, they're not interested in meeting new people,* and
*what should I say?* On and on my mind went. Suddenly
God's grace intervened, and I immediately shut off the
lawn mower, picked up my then-baby daughter, Kyra, who

was playing on the lawn, and began walking across the street. I saw this sea of people on the porch staring right at me, silent as I approached. Then, while I was walking, I began to think again—*What am I doing? Am I crazy? I don't know them! They're probably thinking, who is this guy?* But I kept walking. Sure enough, an hour later, my daughter was out back playing with their kids, and I was frolicking with the group and sipping my second margarita. I didn't need to think my way out of my fear. I needed to act in spite of it.

4. **Fear means you're on the right track. No fear means you're not stretching enough.** Keep in mind, whenever a fear arises, that in 95% of cases, it does not mean you're doing the wrong thing; it means you are moving into an area of growth. It is almost always a positive move. Let your fear inform you that you need to stretch. If you're afraid of asking for a raise, perhaps you need to stretch yourself to face authority figures and ask confidently for what you want. If you're afraid of talking to your spouse about an issue that bothers you in your marriage, perhaps you need to stretch yourself to face the possibility of rejection head-on. In both of these cases, fear only arises because you are moving into a new, uncharted territory—and that is a good thing.

5. **Go 80% of the way the first time.** If all else fails, don't do the thing you fear—do only *part* of the thing you fear. I remember using this technique with

my son Jeremy. When he was very young, he was petrified of dark movie theatres. This began with the movie *Shrek*. As soon as the huge green ogre busted onto the movie screen in the opening sequence, he literally threw his popcorn up in the air and ran out of the theater. But he also loved watching movies—at home. And since his older sister still loved going to the movies, he faced the prospect of having to stay home while his sister watched a new movie—something unthinkable to a younger brother in a competitive sibling rivalry. What to do?

My wife and I broke him of his fear by telling him that he didn't need to sit down in the theater. I would stand with him in the very back of the theater by the door as the lights went down and the movie began. He could run out at any time, stay in the back, or, if he so chose, go sit down. During the first movie we tried this with, Jeremy stayed in the back for 50% of the movie, inched up closer to the seats by the end, and finally sat down just before the closing credits. By the second movie, he was sitting down at the halfway point. By the third movie, he forgot his fear entirely.

Adults can try this technique as well. If you can do just a part of what you fear, it is very likely that you'll take nearly all of the negative emotion out. The air will escape from your fear balloon, and you'll have gone 90% of the way to mastering the fear.

As I've said, probably no time since the Great Depression has our culture needed models of people who can confidently face their fears—and become hopeful role models for others. Use your own life as a school to face and move through your fears, one by one, and then maybe someday you can play a part in leading our culture beyond the era of terror to the era of hope.

# 10

# Enter Your Day Slowly

———◆·◆·◆———

THE SECRET WEAPON OF THE TOP 1%

Several years ago, I had the great opportunity to work with the legendary speaker and author Dr. Ken Blanchard. Ken is one of the best examples of a person with the habits, skills, and attitudes of the Top 1%. You might know Ken as the co-author of one of the top selling business books of all time, *The One Minute Manager*. Ken was not only one of the kindest people I have ever met, but one of the most gifted. While working with him on an audio program called "Personal Excellence," I was astonished at how he could go into the studio and deliver a thirty-minute audio session off the cuff from just a few notes—barely making any errors along the way.

Even more astonishing was Ken's attitude during the often-arduous two-day period that it takes to record an audio program. Even the best of authors gets pretty tired and cranky after a full day of recording alone in a cold studio. But Ken was laughing and jovial during the entire process—and when I called it quits at 5 p.m. the first day, he seemed as if he could have kept going until the sun had set. At dinner that night, I remember asking Ken what his secret was to such a sharp mind and a calm and peaceful demeanor. He said that, in addition to his deep Christian faith and loving spouse, he had a secret that kept him at the top of his game every day: *He entered his day slowly.*

Ken told me that too many people lead frantic, rushed, and overscheduled lives in our 24/7 world. Given the fact that he told me this nearly twenty years ago, we can assume that the frantic pace he was referring to has been taken to a whole new level. But, he acknowledged, he wasn't immune to this frantic pace. As the head of a highly successful training and development company, a bestselling author, and one of the most in-demand speakers in the nation, looking at his schedule book was enough to make anyone dizzy. But, he said, he could handle everything that happened after 7 a.m. as long as he nurtured his source of strength *before* 7 a.m. That source of strength was his mind.

I understood exactly where he was coming from. I have been fortunate to be a morning person all of my life. I can't wait to wake up in the morning—I feel a sense of new beginnings, every problem from the day before takes on a new and positive perspective, and I am full of energy.

I am well aware that not everyone shares my enthusiasm for the morning. For some, any hour prior to 9 a.m. is meant not to be seen but dreamt about. My wife is one of those "night owls" who can be seen reading a magazine with a dim light on at the last stroke of midnight (if she can hear herself think over my snores).

Let me make a radical assertion: *the strategy of entering your day slowly is even more powerful, indeed more necessary, for night owls.* That's because night owls are even more prone to starting off the day on the wrong side of the bed than we annoying morning Pollyannas. So, if you are a night owl, listen on. I think I can convince you that getting up early, albeit in a different way than you are used to, will be even more valuable than that little bit of extra sleep followed by a frantic dash to the shower. You'll see that entering your day slowly is the key to nurturing your mental powers—the genesis of your genius. And it's a secret weapon of the Top 1%.

What do I mean exactly by entering your day slowly? In my mind, three essential elements are required. If you take these three elements into consideration, you can then customize the idea to your personal interests and habits.

First, you need to arise at least one hour prior to when you need to begin getting ready for the day. Two hours is even better, but one hour is a *minimum*. Again, I don't mean one hour before you need to leave for work (if you work in an office) or begin work (if you work from home). I mean a solid one to two hours before you even begin your daily habits of getting ready—breakfast, showering, dressing, et cetera.

Second, if at all possible, this must be "alone time." I know that this is easier said than done, especially if you have young children. But I have managed to maintain this habit for my entire adult life, with three kids. Although they are now self-sustaining teenagers, at one time they were energetic toddlers, so I know it can be done. Alone time is critical for you to be able to recharge your batteries and effectively listen to the inner stirrings of your soul. Such alone time will reap huge dividends during the other waking hours of the day, not only from the standpoint of personal effectiveness, but in your ability to relate to and serve other people. You cannot serve others effectively when your fuel reserves are on empty.

Third, and finally, at least a portion of this time must be devoted to quiet, meditative reflection. Again, depending on your personality and beliefs, this can take many forms: prayer, meditation, writing in your journal, taking a walk as the sun comes up, or just sitting in silence. Do this for at least fifteen minutes upon waking. Why is this so important? It sets the tone for the day by quieting and focusing the mind. Try it for yourself. You will be astonished at the difference this makes.

As long as you apply those three elements to entering your day slowly, you can customize the idea to meet your own personal interests and habits. For example, here is my routine. I get up at 5 a.m. on weekdays and 6 a.m. on weekends. Obviously, to do this and get the sleep I need, I need to be in bed by at least 10 p.m. the night before. But that gives me a solid two hours before I have to begin getting ready in the morning. I arise, put the coffee on, and while the house is filling with the sumptuous aroma of dark roast, I spend the first fifteen minutes in silent prayer and meditation. Then, with a fresh and focused mind, I spend the next hour reading several of my favorite newspapers, magazines, and books—*The Wall Street Journal, The New York Times,* my local paper, various news and opinion blogs, the newest nonfiction best seller. Then I head out for a quick run. When I return, not only do I feel refreshed and energized, but I am ready to take on the day. That's when I begin the morning routine—packing lunches for our two high-school teenagers, getting my wife up for her workday, eating breakfast, showering, et cetera.

But that's just *my* routine. My wife, for example, as a human resources manager, would rather come up with ideas to improve the benefits for her company's employees, or go for a fast walk and think through the day ahead. And that's fine. The key is that it should, as much as possible, be full of low-stress activities that leave your mind fresh and your spirit ready to embrace the day ahead.

Take this idea and customize it for your own life, and judge the results for yourself. I think you'll find, as I have, that a day entered slowly is a mind's best friend.

# 11

# The Prescription
# for Peak Performance

One of my favorite enduring childhood memories is the camping trips I used to take with my dad, as part of what was then called the Indian Guides program (that was the YMCA's version of Boy Scouts). We built model rocket ships (most of which didn't launch), sang around the campfire, went on scavenger hunts, raced canoes, and slept in tents—even during the worst thunderstorms imaginable. But probably my favorite memory is the movie nights at the mess hall on Fridays. My dad and I carried this responsibility for the tribe, and we never failed to pick a movie that was a total hit.

The best movie night we ever had was when we selected the old Laurel and Hardy classic *The Perfect Day*. If you're a Laurel and Hardy fan, this movie needs no introduction. But for anyone not so blessed, this movie certainly warrants a stream on Netflix or Amazon Prime, or a rental (if you can find it on DVD). It is a hilarious comedic sequence of a day that was anything but perfect. Laurel and Hardy endure one miscue after another—falling into mud pits, bumping into one another, showing up at the wrong places, cars breaking down, and ending up with a look of exhaustion and surrender—all with the slapstick, perfectly timed comedic routines that made Laurel and Hardy famous. All of us—fathers and sons alike—ended up laughing so hard it hurt!

As I prepared to write this chapter on peak performance and reflected back on that precious memory, I was struck by how many of us long for the perfect day—the day where everything seems to click. We feel great, we look good, every interaction we have with others is a study in masterful communication and persuasion, we close the big deal at work, we come home and kiss our significant other at night after watching the sunset in our hammock in the backyard. And all without breaking a sweat!

For most of us, such dreams are just that, and our actual days are anything but perfect. Our goals don't seem to come easily, the deal never closes fast enough—at least not fast enough for our boss, if it closes at all. We never seem to get up early enough to work out, especially since our two-year-old started teething. We come home to our spouse intent on having a relaxing night, and we're reminded about the leaky faucet in the bathroom that needs fixing. Yep, most of our "perfect days" seem to be closer to that of Laurel and Hardy than Ozzie and Harriet.

What's even more maddening is that from afar, we look up to other peak performers—be they neighbors, friends, public figures, or celebrities—and we wonder how they seem to do it all, and with seemingly very little effort. How does our friend Jane manage a staff of fifty at her company, raise three kids, swim in triathlons, and still attend PTO meetings? Oh, and at forty, still look like she's thirty? How does Tony Robbins write books, do seminars around the world, coach presidents and CEOs, and run several companies? How can I ever hold a candle to that?

The first notion I want to dispel is the idea that peak performance is about perfection. It is not. To be part of the Top 1%, you don't have to be superhuman. What you don't know is that your neighbor, Jane, secretly wishes she could switch jobs, but feels trapped because of her financial commitments. She also worries about whether she sees her kids enough, especially in their early years. And she's longing to build a deeper connection with her spouse, Jeff—a connection that they had during college but has fizzled because they have spread themselves too thin.

And what you don't know about personal development celebrities like Tony Robbins, and other top personal development experts that I've had the good fortune to work closely with, is that they too have down days and pay a price for their commitments. Their tight travel schedules, public personas, and endless commitments often rob them of the simple pleasures and balance that you and I might take for granted.

No, *peak performance* and the words *perfection* and *effortless* do not belong in the same sentence. In fact, truth be told, the words *perfection* and *effortless* have no place in a discussion about achieving at one's highest potential. Strive for peak performance and high achievement in any area of life, and there is a price to be paid. The key is paying that price *consciously*. I have no doubt that Tony Robbins and our mythical Jane character, despite their occasional misgivings, wouldn't have their lives any other way. They accept their imperfect lives as a necessary consequence of their great performance.

Now that we've discarded the idea of perfection as a key to peak performance, what is the key? While I do not believe in any single reason for anything (life is too complex for that), I do believe that there is a factor that accounts for 90% of peak performance. That factor is energy. Peak performers are, as a rule, high-energy people who have learned to manage the expenditure of their energy very effectively and efficiently.

Think of most of the peak performers you know. How many of them are low-energy, laid-back types? There are a few, but I would argue that they are the exception rather than the rule. And by *high-energy*, I do not necessarily mean the "bouncing off the walls" type. I also mean those who have a high energy stream bubbling under the surface— and who can bring that energy to manifest incredible levels of focus, determination, and willpower. Remember, it is the *management* of energy that is the key. High-energy people who burn both ends of the stick all too often sabotage their ability to sustain peak performance by burning themselves out too fast.

I need to go no further than myself as a perfect example. Many people who know me well have described me as a bundle of energy that runs 24/7. My own wife used to marvel at how I could go to sleep at midnight, get up at 4:30 in the morning, go running, work, and still come home bouncing off the walls with enthusiasm. But on the negative side, I have also endured three bouts with pneumonia, and for a long time I struggled with anxiety issues. In my wife's words, this was God's way of forcing me to slow down.

It could also be said it was God's way of getting me to take notice of my energy management. As a result, I've made several changes in my life—making sure I get seven hours of sleep, reducing my commitments to things that are not top priorities, and focusing on living one day at a time. As a result, I've not lost one iota of my energy level, and I'm calmer and more focused than I've ever been. And I rarely feel burnt out.

I compare the idea of energy management to that of a great pitcher on a baseball team. Pitchers typically play once every five days. What's more, even if a pitcher is pitching a great ball game, a manager will rarely let him finish the game himself; he almost always brings in a relief pitcher in the eighth or ninth inning. Why? Energy management. Studies show that most pitchers' effectiveness drops considerably after 100 pitches—even if their self-evaluation is that they feel strong and can finish the game. And the rest between games ensures that their arms will be in top form for peak performance the next time.

What are some tips you can follow to maximize and manage your energy? Well, keeping with my perfect day theme, I'd like to give you a recommended list of "to dos" for tomorrow, to create your own perfect day—where you feel and perform great:

1. **Enter your day slowly.** I covered this topic in the last chapter, but it bears repeating. Get up at least one hour before you need to begin getting ready for the day, and spend that time reading, meditating, or gently exercising. If that means going to bed a bit earlier, do it. You won't believe the difference that this extra time to yourself makes in your energy level.

2. **Eat a nutritious breakfast.** Studies show that people who regularly eat a balanced breakfast have significantly higher energy and greater overall health. They maintain their ideal weight and have lower blood pressure and cholesterol than those who do not eat breakfast. And since you're entering your day slowly, you'll have plenty of time to eat it!

3. **Put together your Vital Six list.** Before getting to the office or beginning work for the day, follow the late, great Earl Nightingale's advice and write out the six most important things you need to accomplish for the day. List them in order of their importance. Then begin the day by going to work on the first item, and work until it is complete. Then work through the list, one by one, until all of the tasks are complete. While you won't always get through the entire list (because of meetings and other unforeseen, unexpected happenings which always pop up in professional life), the focus this will give to your life and the increased productivity you will experience will serve to both manage and maximize your energy at the same time. It will help you focus like

a laser beam on the essential things, and you'll feel great because of the greater control you have established over your life.

4. **Take a fifteen-minute meditation, prayer, or nap break.** There is no one who can be "on" all the time. You need to be able to recharge your batteries in-between the achievements of your Vital Six list. At some point, preferably midday, take fifteen minutes to meditate, pray to your God, or just take a snooze. Many of the best peak performers I have ever met, like Ken Blanchard, author of *The One Minute Manager,* are worldclass nappers. In fact, Ken has gotten so good at it that one day when I was driving him to the airport, as I turned my head to look out the window, his head bobbed forward. Startled, I looked over, and there he was snoozing for our ten-minute drive to O'Hare. By the time we got there, he popped up and hugged me good-bye as if nothing had happened. There was energy management at its finest!

5. **Finally, don't force-feed positive thoughts.** There's a great deal of misinformation in the self-help industry that says the key to peak performance is maintaining a positive outlook or positive thoughts at all times. This philosophy is totally unsupported by science. Scientific research, unveiled by many, including the late Paul Pearsall in his book *The Last Self-Help Book You'll Ever Need,* finds that achievers don't necessarily think positively all the time. In fact, research has found that the energy and stress

required to force-feed positive thoughts all the time, despite the situation and our true feelings, can lead to incredible highs and sudden, depressive lows. The key to energy management is to acknowledge our feelings, be they good or bad, nervous or calm, joyous or melancholy, and let them pass through us like a flowing river. The key is to not get stuck in unproductive emotions. But don't avoid them. Even bad feelings and emotions can be the grist for a positive change in your life.

Tomorrow it's inevitable that you will encounter challenges and uncomfortable thoughts. It's your challenge to experience those emotions and learn from them, so your energy remains high.

Follow this perfect day prescription, and you can turn any imperfect day into an opportunity for peak performance.

# 12

# The Root System

Snapshot 1998. The dot-com boom is in full swing. Record numbers of millionaires are being created daily. Valuations on paper mean as much, if not more, than real bottom-line profits. Unemployment is around 4%, near a record low. Enron is one of the largest, most respected, and seemingly profitable companies in the world. "Free agency" is the buzzword. People are brands, and company loyalty is out. New financial book releases include *The 401(k) Millionaire, The Long Boom,* and *The Roaring 2000s.* Baby boomers plan on retiring early so they can spend more time with their grandchildren, travel, volunteer for a nonprofit, and just enjoy life. Gen Xers plan on being rich before they're thirty. And those in Generation Y wonder if college is even necessary or if they should start their businesses right away, like the new economy heroes Bill Gates, Steve Jobs, and Michael Dell. That huge Millennial generation is still in diapers. After the Gulf War swiftly ended, the United States has had nearly eight years of peace and prosperity. The future is clear.

Snapshot 2003. Dot-coms have become "dot bombs." Record numbers of former millionaires have seen their net worth shrink faster than an ice cube under hot water. Enron is bankrupt, morally and fiscally. Valuations are held to a new standard: the true bottom line. And if your job doesn't contribute to the bottom line, you're likely on the street. Loyalty is in, and former free agents are spurned by HR departments because they are seen as "job hoppers." New financial books include *The Great 401(k) Hoax, Conquer the Crash,* and Suze Orman's *Protection Portfolio.* Baby boomers face the fact that they may have to retire later, or for some, may never retire fully. Generation Xers are facing salary freezes, and those in Generation Y wonder if they'll be able to afford college and if there will be jobs available when they get out. The Twin Towers have fallen, and Gulf War II is over (we think). The future is unclear. Real estate is one of the few bright spots in the economy.

Snapshot 2010. Coming off the Great Recession, that one bright spot of real estate has gone bust. Baby boomers are putting off retirement; Gen Xers are in the prime of their careers, facing unprecedented levels of change because of increasing levels of high-tech automation and the digitization of our economy. Generation Y has to deal with the realization that they may not just have several jobs during their lifetime, but several careers. And those Millennials? They are long out of diapers and considered "digital natives"—going through their adolescence and college years with smartphones, social media—and cannot imagine a world where every conceivable form of information is not instantly accessible. And that's all before Siri came on the scene.

At the beginning of the twentieth century, the three snapshots I've outlined above would have been no closer than fifty years apart, and that's being generous. In fact, even though we have lived through the changes I outlined above, it still seems almost inconceivable that such changes occurred within five to seven years of each other.

This is just a preview of things to come. *The Futurist* magazine ran a full-length article from a leading futurist, Ray Kurzweil, describing an event he called "the Singularity." The article made the case that change is increasing at such a fast pace that at a time in the not-too-distant future—about 2030—we will reach a point where change happens so fast that we can no longer reliably forecast future events from day to day. According to the article, the critical skill to success in the future (and therefore a skill that those who hope to be part of the Top 1% would do well to develop) would necessarily be *ultimate flexibility*— the ability to change one's perspective and approach at a moment's notice.

It's no wonder then, that as I write these words in 2016, so many people have been asking themselves a very common question due to the sense of disorientation they feel from unprecedented levels of change: *What do I do now?* I'm an entrepreneur and the needs of my customers have changed radically. They are no longer buying what we have to offer. *What do I do now?* I have been laid off from a major software company. The tech industry is just not hiring. *What do I do now?* I'm five years from retirement and my 401(k) is down 50%. *What do I do now?* My family is growing, and I'm in the prime of my career, but my salary has been frozen for over two years. *What do I do now?*

These are legitimate questions with no quick, short term answers. However, there is a larger, longer-term answer to that question that will serve you well, now and well into the future. *What you need to do now is to develop and nurture your root system.*

What exactly do I mean by a root system? I mean a strong set of foundational principles and practices that never change, which serve to nourish you amid times of rapid and unexpected change. Stephen Covey said it best in his classic book *The Seven Habits of Highly Effective People*: "If down deep there is a part of you that doesn't change, you can master the changes in the surface of your life; but if down deep you are continually changing, you'll flop about."

In other words, like an oak tree, you need to have a root system that feeds you when the winds of change, and the occasional hurricanes of disruption, serve to break you. Your task is to bend with the changes, while remaining firm in your convictions—your roots.

I have come up with three roots that can serve to feed us and keep us on solid footing in any economic, societal, or cultural environment.

1. **Nurture a close network of family and friends.**
Many people who have been laid off or seen their
businesses go under in a rough economic climate
have discovered the truth that many have forgotten:
business is business. Ultimately it is not a family,
an identity, or a social life. Because of the incredible demands placed on employees and entrepreneurs
by businesses in order to effectively compete, people
have spent more time working and have, over time,
insidiously, forgotten this truth.

Your spouse, children, extended family, and close friendships must be nurtured on a regular basis. In an increasingly
transient world, where people switch jobs and addresses
with greater frequency, the only constant in our lives will be
the people we love and care about. Not only will they give
us a shoulder to cry on and be in our cheering section when
we go after our greatest goals, they will give us a chance to
contribute to their lives in ways much more meaningful
than can be provided by purely economic transactions.

Yet, sadly, this is the first area that goes by the wayside
when the demands of the marketplace come calling. You
must find creative ways to put the marketplace on hold at
times to make time for those you love.

2. **Study and practice your spiritual tradition.**
Catholicism, Protestantism, Judaism, Buddhism,
Islam, Hinduism, Taoism—the list goes on and on.
Experts say that, in addition to the major religions,
there are over 1000 smaller religions and philosoph-

ical frameworks that encompass our globe. Even for those who don't believe in God, or the traditional understanding of God, there are philosophical "religions," if you will, like Humanism.

With the diversity of religious practice in our culture, it's obvious that we have hit on a vital human need—a need that has persisted for thousands of years—from hunter gatherer, agrarian, industrial, into information economies. Unfortunately, for many, this need is somewhat unconscious and does not get proper attention. People might check in for their spiritual service once a week, say general rote prayers or profess their spiritual beliefs when chatting with friends, but it is the rare person who has integrated their spiritual life at the deepest level of their being by making it a matter of serious study and conscious daily practice.

Regardless of your definition of God, or even your belief in the existence of God, as M. Scott Peck said in *The Road Less Traveled,* everyone has a religion. Make the study of your religion more conscious and frequent. Perform some daily ritual associated with your religious tradition every day after you wake up. Get involved at your place of worship or association at a deeper level. Volunteer. Grow these roots deep. They will be there to inspire you to a mission that transcends the temporal world—giving you the fuel to push toward your goals. What's even more important, they will be there to sustain you when times of great suffering or confusion serve to make you question the very meaning of existence.

3. **Multi–Track Your Career.** There was a popular saying as our parent's generation was growing up, which is still repeated today by many personal development speakers: "Put all of your eggs in one basket, and then watch that basket." In my opinion, this is the advice of a bygone era that, economically speaking, no longer makes sense. Best-selling author and speaker Robert Allen has captured the new approach to personal economics practiced by the Top 1% in the title of his best-selling Nightingale-Conant audio program: *Multiple Streams of Income.* You need to establish income from a variety of sources, preferably passive income, so that if one or two dry up, the others continue to flow.

Even if the Singularity, as futurists have conceived it, is a long way off, there can be no doubt that the changes you face next year will be more extreme than those you are currently facing. Any job or business will be more vulnerable under such conditions. Rather than purely fighting to stay "indispensable" or "one step ahead of the competition," it is even more important to put your eggs in a few baskets of potential income-producing ventures. Perhaps you can turn your hobby into a side business or buy and rent a piece of real estate. Or it can be as simple as keeping your job potential on several tracks through effective networking, so if your job goes south for an economic winter, your professional development opportunities will land you safe in a new job where the economic season is just warming up.

Take these ideas to heart. Make a concerted effort, for thirty days, to instill these ideas into your daily way of thinking, living, and acting. Grow your roots deep, and the winds of change will never break you. You will bend with them and face the sun.

# 13

## The Problem Solvers

———◆·◆·◆———

September 11, 2001, is a day that Americans will never forget. The carnage that resulted from the greatest terrorist attack in our nation's history is so well documented that I don't need to elaborate on it any further.

This fateful day was the day that we suffered a loss of innocence as a nation. Indeed, the challenges faced by our nation since then, and by other nations around the world, seem to have multiplied to such a degree that the '90s look like the era of Camelot by comparison.

While we all remember 2001, many people forget the many challenges our nation suffered in 2005. During that year, the incredibly brave and dedicated men and women of our armed forces continued to stave off the insurgency in Iraq, with no clear end in sight. The city of New Orleans was hit by the largest natural disaster ever with Hurricane

Katrina, and hurricanes took a major toll on cities, sub-urbs, and rural areas alike in Mississippi and Florida. Oil and natural gas prices had skyrocketed, the stock market had been in a perpetual holding pattern, and warnings about avian flu were rampant.

By 2008, the stock market was no longer in a holding pattern; it had crashed. Real estate prices plummeted, and foreclosures were skyrocketing. Consumer confidence was at an all-time low. As I write this in 2016, while the economy has stabilized, many people still feel a sense of unease. Businesses continue to deal with the greatest paradox in modern times: to stay competitive globally, outsourcing has practically become a necessity, but at the same time, outsourcing is posing a threat to individual careers and in some ways to how competitive the United States will be in the future. If it weren't for the fact that my favorite team, the Notre Dame Fighting Irish, went all the way to the Elite Eight, I would call it "the year that tested my mettle."

Yet, in the face of all of these challenges and many more, I haven't lost one shred of my optimism about the future. And neither should you. Why? When scores of politicians, economists, special interest groups, and talking heads on "shout TV" programs are busy complaining, assigning blame, and making excuses, it is tempting to believe that our country has lost its edge and that things are teetering on the brink of chaos.

Why am I so optimistic? It's because of a class of individuals that exist in America and to whom our future belongs. *The entrepreneurs.* If you have plans to join the ranks of the

Top 1%, you may want to consider becoming one yourself, if you have not already.

Webster's definition of an entrepreneur is "one who organizes, manages, and assumes the risks of a business or enterprise." Others have even more complex definitions. Bob Reiss, successful entrepreneur and author of *Low Risk, High Reward: Starting and Growing Your Small Business with Minimal Risk,* says: "Entrepreneurship is the recognition and pursuit of opportunity without regard to the resources you currently control, with confidence that you can succeed, with the flexibility to change course as necessary, and with the will to rebound from setbacks."

Look at some of the words used by each of those definitions—*organizes, manages, risks, pursuit, confidence, and rebound.* These are not words that denote passivity. Each of those words conveys an air of proactivity. In fact, if I was to simplify both of those definitions to their very essence, I would define an entrepreneur as "one who enriches his or her life, and the lives of others, by solving problems." Period. The reason I am so confident that we cannot only meet but solve the challenges I discussed earlier, is because entrepreneurs are busy making a living by eagerly looking to solve the problems that plague us.

When the democratic elections took place in Iraq, in addition to our brave men and women in uniform, it was entrepreneurs who rushed to set up businesses and serve a new market of opportunity. And without the work of entrepreneurs, a viable long-term democracy would not even be a remote possibility there. While Americans across the nation have volunteered their time to serve the needy in New Orleans after such a tragedy, it is the entrepreneurs who have been largely responsible for rebuilding the city, establishing new businesses, and ultimately making it into a place once again where people love to live and work. Entrepreneurs worldwide are currently looking into new, renewable energy sources that can liberate our country from our dependency on oil. Entrepreneurs are operating businesses that have developed vaccines to protect human beings from avian flu. And it is entrepreneurs who are trying to provide new, alternate forms of education that will keep our population competitive and ready to address the challenges of a global economy. Yes, many will get rich with their efforts, but by so doing, those who have made integrity their code of conduct will ultimately serve millions of others.

If these large-scale macroeconomic benefits are not reason enough to consider becoming an entrepreneur, there are many microeconomic reasons to do so. First, since corporate downsizing has become the norm and with the rise of outsourcing will continue into the foreseeable future, you really only have two options: (1) quit and become an entrepreneur; or (2) adopt the skills of the entrepreneur and apply them in the workplace.

We'll discuss those skills (or decisions) in a moment, but there really is no third choice. The corporate ladder is gone. Entrepreneurship, either in reality or as a mental paradigm, is the only path to economic security.

Furthermore, in a 24/7 world, it is crucial to have some kind of control over your work schedule in order to maintain any kind of balance in your life. Yes, the tables have turned! Ironically, many of my entrepreneurial friends now have much more flexibility and balance than those of us in corporate America. Without a boss to answer to, they can call their own shots.

Next, an entrepreneurial life is a way to do what you love and make a living at it. I have met very few entrepreneurs who hate what they do and long to get back to the nine-to-five corporate life. Many of them started their businesses around their major personal gifts and passions and built a profitable business plan around them. In fact, *New York Times* columnist Thomas Friedman, in his brilliant classic *The World Is Flat,* discusses the rise of a new type of entrepreneur in our global economy: the socially conscious entrepreneur. Similar to what I described earlier, these are entrepreneurs who are doing what they love by bringing their entrepreneurial skills to solving some of the great economic, health, and social ills of our day.

Finally, countless books on this subject reveal that there is only one regret when it comes to entrepreneurship: *Never having given it a try.* Very few entrepreneurs, even those whose businesses have failed and who have returned to a regular job, regret their decision to become entrepreneurs. Most are like my good friend Don, who after trying and failing at his first entrepreneurial venture, worked in corporate America for a few years, and after learning the lessons from his first failure and gaining some additional business experience, took the entrepreneurial plunge once again. Fourteen years later, he is a major success.

Right about now, I can imagine three questions that might be swirling in your head: (1) Dan, I'm not an entrepreneur right now. What do I need to do to become one? (2) Dan, I'm already an entrepreneur, but I'm not successful. I certainly don't feel like I'm getting any of the benefits you've discussed. Why not? (3) Dan, for several reasons, personal and otherwise, I'm just not going to become an entrepreneur. How can the ideas presented in this chapter help me?

As you'll see in a minute, anyone asking any of these three questions can get value from this chapter.

I'd like to introduce a couple of concepts from one of my favorite authors, coaches, and thinkers on entrepreneurship: Dan Sullivan. In addition to being president of The Strategic Coach—a lifetime coaching company that serves entrepreneurs worldwide—he is also the author of a great audio program, called *Pure Genius,* and a best-selling book, *The Laws of Lifetime Growth.* Dan's ideas have had a considerable influence on my life—in fact he convinced me to take the entrepreneurial path as the president of my own company, Inspire Productions.

According to Dan, anyone can become an entrepreneur (or an "intra-preneur," meaning a person who employs the entrepreneurial mindset as an employee within the boundaries of a company) by making what he calls the *two entrepreneurial decisions.* In fact, Dan asserts, if you make these two decisions and act on them, you already have become an entrepreneur. Here they are:

**Decision Number One:** I will depend entirely on my own abilities for my economic security.

**Decision Number Two:** I will expect no opportunity until I have first created value for someone else.

You can see that, taken to heart, these two decisions would completely change your perspective on the world. Make these decisions and act on them, and you have the foundation of success regardless of the business you choose or the company for which you work.

Be honest with yourself. Even if you are running your own business, have you truly made these two decisions? Do you secretly still operate as if you had a job, and do you expect that just "working hard" should provide you with an income? Does your product or service truly create value for others in the marketplace? Have you differentiated your product or service, or is it one among hundreds of commodities that has no way of standing out in the mind of your customer?

Make these decisions for the first time, or consider them at a deeper and more honest level, and you may have the answers you're looking for to realize greater success in your business.

Finally, can you see how making these decisions as part of a company would separate you from the rest of your peers and land you in the executive suite? How many people in your company truly depend on their own abilities for their economic security versus just expecting that paycheck regardless of what effort and creative thought they put into their job? How could you restructure your pay in your company so you receive 50% or more of your compensation from your own bottom-line results? Can you see how this could take you to a whole different level of economic success and reignite your desire and passion in your job? How can you look for ways to add value to your company, even outside your job description?

You can participate in these entrepreneurial decisions and essentially become an entrepreneur within a corporate structure. The choice is yours. And remember, this is the only choice that will be rewarded in the twenty-first century.

Make these two entrepreneurial decisions to join the ranks of the Top 1%, and become one of the world's fortunate few who make a living, or even become wealthy, not by exploiting, but by solving the problems of humanity.

# 14

# The Dream Job

Reaching the pinnacle of success, the Top 1%, is the stated goal of this book and, I hope, its readers. But certainly a secondary goal is to be able to achieve this through the vehicle of one's dream job. Indeed, it could be said that doing what one loves to do for a career is the very best way to be successful at it. As Confucius once said, "Choose a job you love, and you will never have to work a day in your life."

The idea of the dream job—the goal of nearly every businessperson, be they an employee or an entrepreneur, is one that is emblazoned on our brains since the moment we leave high school and begin to prepare for our careers. This dream job—just like the dream car, the dream house, the dream spouse, or the dream lifestyle—

is always something "out there" to attain. Rarely is it something that we may believe we are close to actually attaining.

Tragically, most people seem to have fallen for the trap that the dream job is for a select few chosen people, something that others, like pro athletes, celebrity actors, or TV personalities, live out right in front of our eyes, but is not something that we likely could ever attain.

But it isn't true. The myth behind the magic is that you don't have to be a celebrity or an athlete to attain your dream job. Your dream job is right within your reach. In fact, there's a good chance it may be right under your feet. The purpose of this chapter is to give you several ideas that you can use to turn the job you now possess, or any job you may pursue in the future, into the job of your dreams. I'm going to save you from the lottery mentality that says you have to be cast in the next *Celebrity Apprentice* to win your dream job, and make you the star of your own reality show—"The Dream Catcher." And I think my approach will leave you far more satisfied.

1. **What is your ultimate dream job?** Write out a description in five sentences of exactly what your dream job would consist of—pay, perks, focus, location, et cetera. Be realistic. When you say "dream job," make sure that the "dream" consists of all the elements of life that are important to you—career growth, family, community, et cetera. In other words, if you think only about the company and job and not the fact that you may be on the road 70–

80% of the time, your dream job may quickly turn into a nightmare because of how it affects the totality of your life. Make sure you take all elements into account.

2. **Survey your current job and position.** How close does it come to the description above? You may be surprised that, particularly when you take your whole life into account, your job may come closer to your dream job than you think. If you determine that your dream job isn't just in another organization, but in your current organization, you have a couple of options.

First is the concept of job shaping. In the current work environment, where talented workers are at a premium, employers are often willing to go to great lengths to retain their best employees. If you like, you can look at the research on this topic in the excellent book *The Loyalty Effect* by Frederick Reichheld and Thomas Teal and published by Harvard Business Review Press. It presents the staggering financial costs involved in replacing mid- to high-level employees in an organization. You can take advantage of this fact. Stand back from your job and look at it like a piece of clay that you can shape and model into its ideal form. Then work with your boss to incorporate more of the elements that would fulfill you, and hence enable you to make a greater contribution to your company, while minimizing or eliminating the aspects of your job that you hate. Or, if you love the organization but are more interested in another area of the company, you can make a lateral move. For example, moving from public relations to marketing or from the sales team to the Internet team. This is a great way to gain more skills while staying at a company you love. Finally, you might love every aspect of your job now, but find that it consumes you—offering you no balance in your life.

Several economists have noted that the '90s were the decade where employees went from quantity of salary (the mantra of the '80s) to quality of life. It was the decade of the Family and Medical Leave Act, job sharing, flexible hours, and telecommuting.

Fortunately for you, now, in the late-2010s, most employers are more attentive to work/life balance and expect that employees will want more flexibility in their jobs to achieve it. You can use this to your advantage. If you love your job but can't remember the last time you kissed your kids before bedtime, you might want to talk to your employer about how to achieve greater balance. Perhaps you could work from home one or two days a week, start earlier and finish earlier, or work four long days, with one day off. The possibilities are endless.

3. **Search for greener pastures.** After analyzing your current industry, company, and position, you might still have the intuition that the grass really is greener elsewhere. But how can you be sure? Paul Zane Pilzer, in his audio program *The Fountain of Wealth,* gave us the answer. He calls it "the 50% rule." When you join a new company or start a new business, quite often 95% of your output is learn-

ing, and 5% of your output is doing things you already know how to do well. After a few months or years, it may be that still 60% of your time is spent learning and 40% is spent doing things you know how to do well. As soon as those lines cross, where 51%, 60%, or, probably, as for most people, 95% of your time is spent doing things you already know well, it's time to move. In an economy that demands growth and contribution, you can't afford to let your skills atrophy—regardless of the size of your paycheck.

Again, fortunately for you, there have never been more resources for jumping ship, not just to a new job, but to your dream job. Since statistics show that 75% of positions are obtained by networking (that statistic is probably even higher when you are going for a dream job that fits you uniquely), this is where you want to start. And via the web, you can access a wide variety of networking resources: associations in your chosen profession, your university alumni database, community and volunteer organizations whose members include many of the most successful leaders in your community—the list goes on and on.

To cover the other 25% of positions, the web has reinvented the want ads. Scores of job websites, like Monster .com, sixfigurejobs.com, indeed.com, and jobs.com, provide not only worldwide listings of jobs in your area, but every type of career and resume advice imaginable, to put you on the right track.

4. **Make a business out of your dream.** You might decide that the dream part of your job is to be your own boss and to eliminate all of the corporate politics. Or you may decide that your dream is so unique, there is no position available that will fit your dream. In that case, you might be called to join the entrepreneurial world and do what entrepreneurs do best: create a unique opportunity. There are scores of resources available just for this purpose, published by the publisher of this book, G&D Media. One of my favorites is *Discover the Entrepreneur Within* by Verinder Syal. It shows you how to create a successful business, step by step, that fits your life.

Whatever resources you choose, if you've eliminated the first three avenues I outlined above, you may be called to be an entrepreneur. Investigate it seriously. It is a unique calling, but it may be the only one that will land you your dream job.

I'd like to close with a personal comment about going for your dreams: *like what you like*. By that I mean don't succumb to the pressure of going for a career opportunity that "looks good" or that everyone else expects you to go for but that doesn't turn you on.

A good friend, who is a Harvard MBA, told me about the extraordinary pressure he felt to "do something big" with his degree and follow the majority of his fellow graduates into the investment banking world. Big money, big prestige, and a big lifestyle awaited him—with just one problem: he hated the thought of becoming an investment banker. His dream was to go into executive search. He founded his own very successful executive search firm. He brought such passion to his business that he has created a search firm with a unique business model that helped to redefine the industry. Remember that you are unique, and you need to live with you twenty-four hours a day. Only you can define what makes you happy.

# 15

# The Templeton Test

HOW THE TOP 1% PREPARE FOR RETIREMENT

I must admit that I'm a bit of an oddball when it comes to accepting what most people refer to as "common sense." For example, I lived in one of the storied "two flats" behind the Cubs' great Wrigley Field in Chicago some twenty-five years ago, during my single days, yet I was a rabid White Sox fan. While the rest of my friends in high school blasted Def Leppard and Twisted Sister, I spent most of my teenage years listening to '70s music (and still do in my late forties). I graduated college having taken only one business course—a required course my freshman year—while focusing all of my other courses in the liberal arts, yet I've spent every moment since my graduation working in business. Politically, my views have never seemed to fit with either major party—I refer to myself as a radical moderate. I listen to talk radio while I work out. I love my toast burnt. Go figure.

So while admitting to my "nonlinear" nature ahead of time, I have to say that I've never understood the financial obsession that Americans have with the idea of retirement. The first time I remember hearing the Statistic was in my high-school consumer ed class. What is the Statistic? You've no doubt heard it repeated in numerous self-help seminars and in nearly every financial book on the market. In fact Earl Nightingale introduced his version of the Statistic on his classic recording *The Strangest Secret*. Based on recent economic data, the Statistic goes like this: *out of 100 people who reach retirement age at sixty-five, four will be financially independent, one will be wealthy, and ninety-five will be broke.*

This statistic has been stated various ways and the numbers have shifted just slightly over the years—mostly in the negative direction. In fact, that's why the goal of this program is to get you into the Top 1%—to guarantee that you never have to worry about retirement, so you can keep your focus on adding value for the precious days you have on this planet.

Admittedly, this statistic has served to wake up the general population to the fact that they need to get their financial house in order. And that's not altogether a bad thing. But there is an important set of questions that every person who is in, or who aspires to be in, the Top 1% needs to face. Has our obsession over preparing financially for our "golden years" cost us something important during our early years? Has the need to be a millionaire by the time we're sixty-five become too important? Has it obscured our ability to live life fully in the present? Most of all, has it served to put too thin a veneer on our retirement—making it purely a financial nirvana in which we live in relaxation and luxury without a care in the world?

Don't get me wrong. I know that financial security and even wealth can be great assets as we reach our retirement years. But they are only assets when placed in a larger context—when we step back and define retirement more broadly. After all, what good are millions of dollars in the bank without loved ones to share it with, without a purpose for which to spend it, without a healthy body and mind to experience it?

About seventeen years ago, I came face-to-face with an incredible man who contradicted nearly everything that I had been taught to believe about retirement. Indeed, he was one of the most impressive members of the Top 1% that I have ever had the opportunity to meet. His name was Sir John Templeton, and he was the founder of what is now Franklin Templeton Investments. Sir John passed away in 2008, but during his ninety-five years, he lived as full a life as one could possibly imagine. During his lifetime, he was one of the richest people on the planet, with a fortune of several billion dollars.

I was fortunate enough to work with Sir John on a product called *The Laws of Inner Wealth,* detailing his philosophy of spiritual abundance. Now here was a man who had more money than millions of people combined. If there was anyone who had earned the right to retire at sixty-five at his home in the Bahamas, relaxing and playing shuffleboard, he was that person. Before I went to his office building in Nassau, Bahamas, I expected a place of opulence, a place where

Sir John was waited on hand and foot by servants. I also anticipated difficulty in completing our project, which was on a tight deadline, given that Sir John was nearly eighty-six years old and probably had better things to do than record an audio program, which I assumed the president of his foundation had coerced him to do.

When I arrived at Sir John's office, I was stunned. It was very nice but hardly opulent. In fact it was very humble, filled with old furniture, an old black analog phone, and a desk stacked with apparent projects in process. The coffee table was filled with current newspapers and magazines—this was a man who was certainly still in touch with what was going on in the world. Then Sir John entered the room, walking briskly with the energy of a twenty-one-year-old, neatly dressed in a light blue suit and tie, and welcoming me with his patented and infectious smile. He extended his hand out to me with a firm handshake and told me how he had been looking forward to recording this program, a chance to discuss the spiritual principles that his foundation, the John Templeton Foundation, was trying to foster in our modern world.

We recorded his segments in just one day—an incredible feat for any author. Sir John was as focused as anyone I had ever worked with. Yet he also knew his limits, taking little cat naps every ninety minutes to restore his high energy level and stamina.

My experience with Sir John altered my view of retirement dramatically. Sir John had more money than most people could ever dream of—ultimate financial security in his retirement years. Yet his energy, focus, and drive at eighty-six was probably no different from when he had founded Templeton Mutual Funds nearly a half century earlier. Far from retiring, Sir John never missed a beat, switching his focus in his elder years to a lifelong passion—helping religion and spirituality to progress at the same level that science had progressed in the past hundred years. To foster this goal, his foundation gives one of the largest charitable awards each year to "a living person who has made an exceptional contribution to affirming life's spiritual dimension."

Before and after our recording, Sir John was briefed on all manner of projects relating to his work at the foundation, and his schedule seemed to be as demanding as that of any corporate CEO. Here I was faced with a living contradiction to what I thought retirement was all about. This man hadn't "retired" from anything; he had merely moved on to an exciting new stage of life.

After this experience, I identified four strategies Sir John followed that, if imitated, will lead to a much richer, more holistic and rewarding retirement for you:

1. **Determine, well ahead of your Golden Age of sixty-five, a larger purpose for your retirement.** This idea is more important than any amount of money you could put away. Sir John had a vision for his foundation which provided him a purpose so strong that it gave him the vitality and focus of a man many years younger.

Statistics show that, regardless of how much money they have, retirement is the most difficult transition most people make in their lives. In fact, post-retirement heart attacks and bouts with depression are extremely common—especially for those who make a sudden shift from work to leisure. Why? It's not that we don't want to slow down at all—even Sir John needed his cat naps. The key is establishing a larger purpose for what is sure to be nearly a third of our life.

2. **Make an even greater investment in your health than you do in your savings account to prepare for your retirement.** Again, according to the statistics, in the near future most people will not, mostly due to financial considerations, be able to retire at the Golden Age of sixty-five. What's more, as I just mentioned, this generation is poised to have the longest retirement on record, with life expectancies skyrocketing because of advancements in medical care. You don't want to spend all those years in a hospital bed, crippled with a major disease, or severely limited in your mobility because you are overweight.

Sir John was a model of health—obviously the fruit of a lifelong obsession. He was fit, trim, and full of energy. Again, he knew his limits and pushed himself right to those limits, but not beyond them. Make an investment in your health now so you can reap the dividends later.

3. **Customize the idea of retirement to one that fits your lifestyle and personality.** There is no fixed formula about when you should retire, how much

money you should have, or what you should do
during your retirement. In fact, for many people the
whole idea of retirement is anathema. They prefer to
just keep doing what they've been doing—why stop
because someone tells you to? Sir John reminded me
of a passage I had read in a profound but unconventional book by Stephen Pollan called *Die Broke,* in
which he chose a new model for retirement—that
of Ulysses. To quote Stephen Pollan, "Rather than
viewing your life as finite, as a climb to an arbitrary
fixed point—age 65—at which you stop, approach
life as an adventure. Like Ulysses, you're on a journey, a trip over hills and through valleys with no
known ending other than death. Don't accept someone else's judgment as to when your trip should end.
Do your own navigation and make your own decisions on your journey to the new economic age." I
couldn't say it better.

4. **Finally, yes, finances do matter.** But, again, they
only matter to the degree that they help you fulfill
your predetermined retirement goals. Forget the
formulas and tables that tell you how much money
you must have to retire comfortably. *You* are in the
driver's seat. Once you determine your own goals,
adjust your investing and savings accordingly. Sir
John's goals were ambitious and required huge assets to execute; yours may be nearly as ambitious, or
more modest. *You* hold the key. Once you cover the
first three steps we've just discussed, this fourth step
become much easier to execute.

So rather than being frightened by the Statistic, it's much more important to ask yourself if you pass the Templeton Test. If not, take a fresh look at your retirement goals. Think of yourself as Ulysses on a grand adventure. Your destination is the Top 1%—and no matter what setbacks or challenges may lie ahead of you, if you stay focused on your goal, staying true to your decision to be uncommonly successful, you will arrive at your destination—as surely as an ocean liner arrives at its port, even though it may be slightly off-course here and there for over 90% of its journey. And, oh yeah, throw out all that useless "common sense" about your retirement. Take it from someone who knows—"common sense" isn't all it's cracked up to be.

# 16

# The Power of Who You Are

Several years ago, after completing my usual Saturday afternoon rituals of lawn mowing, edging, and fertilizing—what some people call "Every Man's Paradise"—I sat down to watch the late Tim Russert's talk show on CNBC. Tim died way too young, and I miss his presence in the world of news reporting. I always respected Tim as one of the fairest, yet toughest, journalists on television. And I considered him to be a welcome relief from the daily fare of shouting bullies who seem to dominate television and radio today.

So on this day I was no doubt surprised when he announced that one of his guests was one of television's most famous shouting bullies, who shall remain nameless, invited 'to debate an economist from the opposite side of the political spectrum. Over the past several years, in profiles about our famous, nameless friend, one of the most common adjectives used to describe this gentleman was "assertive." And, five minutes into the interview, this man wasted no time in living up (or down) to his reputation. I watched in disbelief as he debated the economist by shouting him down, waving fingers in his face, calling him names, and giving him looks of contempt, as an adult might give an errant child.

It was so embarrassing that even Tim Russert looked shocked, and it was one of the few times I witnessed Tim losing control of his show and almost taking sides with the other party, if for no other reason, out of sympathy. What struck me as I watched this charade, before turning off the TV in disgust, was how confused we have become over the difference between genuine assertiveness, of which Tim Russert is a great model, and aggressive, bully-like tactics modeled by our nameless friend.

Unfortunately, the media and our culture overall have moved too far in the direction of the bully model—using shouting, intimidation, ad hominem attacks, and clever debating tricks—as opposed to using genuine civil discourse, or true assertiveness.

Despite this considerable confusion over what true assertiveness is, there is no doubt that learning how to exercise this skill is essential to one's success. In fact, it could be said that learning the skill of assertiveness is the key to showcasing every other skill or talent you have. A high IQ, an exceptional talent or ability, or a great sense of judgment will remain your best-kept secrets if you do not develop the capacity to assert them.

Think of it like the rays of the sun. The sun is always there, yet on a severely cloudy day, its rays are hidden from view, as if they've disappeared. The sun is still releasing all of its heating potential and lighting the sky; it's just hidden from view. Then, all of a sudden, a few of the clouds start to break, and we witness the beautiful sight of the sun's rays bursting through like laser beams and illuminating the countryside. Assertiveness skills give us the ability to appropriately showcase the gifts that we possess, to shine through the cloud cover of our doubts and fears.

As parents, we all recognize how important this can be to our children's future success. I remember eating at Chipotle many years ago with my wife and three children, a Strutzel family favorite to this day. Our daughter, Kyra, then eight years old, was a bit on the shy side, and my wife and I had been doing our best to give her small opportunities to let her personality emerge in public. (If you have kids, you'll agree that kids have no trouble letting their personalities shine forth at home!) When the burritos were prepared, I asked Kyra to go up and pick up the food for us and to ask for some extra hot sauce on the side. Well, you would have thought she was being asked to negotiate a world peace treaty. She hemmed and hawed and, for a while, refused to go up to the counter. After considerable coaxing from Mom and Dad, she finally shuffled up to the counter, head down and arms crossed. My wife and I smiled as she seemed to whisper something to the waitress. The waitress gave her a big smile, dropped the hot sauce on the tray, and winked. Seconds later Kyra skipped back with the food, head up and beaming from ear to ear.

"Here's your hot sauce, Daddy!" she said. My wife and I smiled as we witnessed one tiny breakthrough in Kyra's own assertiveness—a skill that, if she can master it, will serve her well in bringing forth her incredible natural gifts.

There is another aspect of assertiveness that often gets lost but seems to become even more important as we age. Minister and speaker Cal LeMon expressed it with a famous quote: "Assertiveness is not what you do; it's who you are." The core of assertiveness is the true expression of our essence, our uniqueness. In this way, the point of assertiveness is not to bully the other person into agreeing with us or giving us what we want. It is not to become a bigger extrovert than everybody else, or to use manipulative tactics to get noticed for the sake of getting noticed by our superiors. We could achieve all of these goals and still fail Cal LeMon's test of revealing our true self.

No, to be truly assertive is more a process of protecting who we are. It is learning certain specific skills that enable us to succeed in everyday life, without compromising our integrity or giving away our essence.

We often wonder why little children who seem so confident and expressive at age two and three often become so lifeless and conformist as teenagers and young adults. Often, whether it's being in the "in group" in high school, or starting to climb the ladder in your first job out of college, the maxim seems to be nothing other than to fit in.

Sadly, too many people never move beyond this stage of fitting in. They end up compromising so much over time that they no longer know what they believe or who they are. This is also why, as people age, even the most introverted among us tend to naturally become more assertive. The older we get, the less we can tolerate conforming for the sake of conforming, and we begin to reclaim our essence in order to leave our own unique stamp on the world. And of course our goal in getting you to the Top 1% is not to follow a path that requires you to compromise your integrity or your true self. Rather it is to make your mark on the world by more fully expressing your uniqueness.

My main message to you in this chapter is, don't wait until you can no longer tolerate giving away your true self. Begin today to practice true assertiveness by protecting who you are. Here are a few ideas that will help you to achieve that goal.

1. **Learn to say "no."** If you are going to achieve your highest priorities in life, it is vital that you learn to say "no" to those things that do not take you in the direction of those priorities. As Stephen Covey says, It is easy to say 'no' to insignificant things, "when there is a larger 'yes' burning inside of you." Get clear on your top five priorities over the next year, and get good at saying no to the activities and urgencies imposed by others that do not take you in the direction of those priorities.

2. **Apply your "matchless self" to every task you undertake.** I'm indebted to the late Wayne Dyer, author of some of the best-selling books in history on self-actualization and spirituality, for introducing me to this life-changing concept. In essence, it means to perform every activity in your own unique

way, resisting the temptation to follow the crowd. Whether it's cooking dinner, negotiating a business deal, taking a family vacation, writing a poem, or raising your children, give it your own unique flair. Resist following the same sanitized, conveyor-belt approach if it does not suit you.

3. **Always clarify the truth of every situation.** It is very common, both in your career and your personal life, for people—be they your boss, your friends, or your spouse—to put words in your mouth about how you feel, what you like, or what you believe. And far too often their assessment is wrong. Make a point to always clarify the truth of your feelings, likes, and beliefs when you are being misrepresented. If we fail to do this, we are giving away a piece of ourselves to others. Do it respectfully, but let others know where you truly stand. I love what the late inspirational speaker Leo Buscaglia used to say: "When you go to heaven God is not going to ask you why you didn't do as well as others or think like others did; his only admonishment will be—'*Why didn't you become you?*'"

4. **Learn to dissent without being disagreeable.** Life presents various situations where you will be out of sync with the group consensus, where everyone in your department, family, or neighborhood will be unified in their agreement on a given issue, except for you. In most cases, the single dissenting party will remain silent, or, worse, act as if they are in agreement. Don't let this be you. Experiment with

respectful and honorable ways of dissenting, even when it seems that the consensus is against you. God created you with a unique mind and a unique perspective. Not to share it is to rob your department, your family, or your neighborhood of a great gift.

Practice these skills and you won't have to bully others to accept your point of view or manipulate others to get noticed. The power of who you are will attract others to you.

# 17

# Solution-Based Selling

THE KEY SKILL OF THE TOP 1%

"The era of sales is over." This is the mantra that began to be heard during the mid-'90s in the midst of the dot-com boom and continues today in the increasingly automated, mobile, and consumer-driven world of the 2010s. The theory is that, increasingly, people are not going to have to deal with those tricky salespeople or be manipulated and cajoled into buying. The Internet has changed all of that. With the click of a mouse, in the privacy of their homes and businesses, customers can make their own decisions, and even the best sales pitch can be resisted by clicking "no thanks" on a banner ad. New companies like CarMax have built their whole business model around "no hassle" salespeople who aren't on commission and are there "just to help."

Indeed, many companies seem to act as if the "we won't try to sell you anything" strategy is a sure ticket to big sales!

But, like sugar-free, store brand ice cream, the promise of the "no selling" strategy has left me with a bad aftertaste. I'm longing for the real thing. We no longer have salespeople, so we now have e-mail boxes filled with spam and banner ads that we can't click off. I no longer have to be "sold" an insurance policy, so now I have to sift through scores of policies, figure out which ones make sense, and do all the research when I could be spending time with my wife at the latest wine-tasting event in town, or watching my sons at their next seven-on-seven football practice. I no longer have to haggle with that salesperson, so I can now pay a flat, inflexible amount for my car, and I can't even use my skills to get them to throw in some free oil changes for the deal. No, we didn't need to get rid of salespeople; we just needed to go from the store brand to the Häagen-Dazs version—*the solution based salesperson.*

Many have rightly reacted against the salespeople who are still stuck with the old sales techniques from a bygone era—those techniques that sought to impose a predetermined product or service on an unsuspecting customer. The rules have changed, driven partly by the Internet, but mostly by the customer, who is increasingly more educated about his or her choices. Most customers would gladly trade spending all their free time sifting through their own sales choices for many products and services—be they financial services, cars, electronics, or homes—if they knew they were dealing with a salesperson who was a trusted advisor, leading them to a solution that fit their needs and values.

The key issue here, of course, is trust. Many experts on the consultative selling process agree that the whole idea of closing the sale has become almost irrelevant. If the salesperson has done his or her job by matching product or service with the needs, wants, and values of the client, the close should be no more than "why don't we move forward?" I would trade my afternoon searching hundreds of life insurance companies and policies for one life insurance salesperson that I could completely trust. And I know I am not alone.

Now you may be thinking to yourself, "I'm not in the profession of sales, and I'm not interested in selling." Even if you *are* in the profession of selling, you may ask what it has to do with reaching the Top 1%. Simply this. The skill of sales, and in particular "solution-based" selling, is *the* key skill you must develop (whether you label your profession as "sales" or not) in order to significantly increase your income, your overall net worth, and most of all, your effectiveness as a human being. As Arthur "Red" Motley, publisher of *Parade* magazine, said way back in 1942: "Nothing happens until somebody sells something." Whether you are selling a product, an idea, your skills, your business, or yourself—effectiveness starts and ends with selling.

Several years ago, when developing a new program, *The Dale Carnegie Leadership Mastery Course,* along with the Dale Carnegie organization, we made a startling assertion: the era of the Internet, e-mail, and increasingly "virtual" types of communications would make human relations skills even *more* of a critical skill in the future.

Many experts were asserting just the opposite—what with e-mail and other non-face-to-face communications, one-on-one human relations skills were going to diminish in importance. But think of it. In an increasingly virtual world, more and more people are becoming very rusty in the area of human relations. They simply are out of practice. Can you imagine how much more of a competitive edge you would have if you were to become an expert in this area? You would stand out far more than you would in generations past, when face-to-face communication was commonplace.

The fact is, we are social creatures. Video sales didn't diminish movie theater sales, and bigger homes with high-tech kitchens have not stopped people from filling restaurants on weekends. The same is true for the sales profession and selling skills. Top level, Häagen-Dazs-quality salespeople, I predict, will be even more valuable in the future. But they will need to be a new breed of salesperson—a high-trust salesperson. Yes, the Internet will easily replace sales where little trust is required—paying utilities, booking a hotel or airline reservation, et cetera. But in the areas where a great deal of knowledge and investment is involved, there will always be a place for high-trust, top-notch salespeople.

Whether you sell for a profession or are just selling your ideas to others, how can you increase your trust level with other people? I have some very good suggestions from Todd Duncan, the top sales trainer and best-selling author of *High Trust Selling*.

In his newsletter, *Sales Wired,* he suggests that to have—and keep—a heart for those to whom you sell and serve, ask yourself the following three questions before entering each new sales relationship.

1. **Can I be fulfilled serving this person?** It's an important question, because if you do not share the same values as the person to whom you're selling, there will be problems down the road, if not immediately. If you wouldn't be proud bringing a potential client "home to mama" or introducing a potential client to your closest friends, then chances are pretty good that a relationship with them will be nothing but heartache.

2. **Does what I sell provide this person the best solution?** If you aren't selling something that is truly top-of-the-line, start selling something that is. That doesn't mean you need to get a new job selling the most expensive product in your field. If you're selling an average car with world-class service and an unbeatable warranty, then sell the service and the warranty—and tell the client what he is getting. Don't ever misrepresent your product or service. If you're in the business of being dishonest, get out of the sales profession. You're doing no one any good— especially yourself.

3. **Is what I offer along this person's current life path?** Don't make the sales profession a game of convincing people to change their values or desires. Listen to what a potential client is telling you, then determine if buying from you will move her down the path she values most. If your heart is in the right place, you will want to confirm her deepest values and meet her deepest desires with the product or service you offer.

Whether you're selling a product, service, or an idea (like your own business), ask yourself these questions and you'll not only be trusted, you'll be part of the new sales revolution, and you'll have fun proving all those "new economy" soothsayers wrong!

# 18

# The Fuel That Never Runs Dry

Philosophers and poets throughout the ages have been searching for the secrets to happiness and fulfillment. Anyone who's interested in the topic can take a trip to their local Barnes & Noble, or go online to Amazon.com, and spend hours reading through scores of titles, old and new, on the perfect recipe for living life to the fullest. But if you're like me, you know that there is a world of difference between reading about something and actually experiencing it. It was Mark Twain who said, "I'm an old man and I've had many troubles, most of which have never happened." I'd like to add to that adage, "I'm a middle-aged man and I've lived many happy and successful days, most of which have never happened."

Don't get me wrong. I love life, and I consider myself to be as positive as they come. But I also know how easy it is to read or listen about success and fantasize that this process is the same as actually living a happy and successful life. They are not the same. Ideas must be supplied by action. Fortunately, I've discovered the perfect laboratory where the secret to happiness and fulfillment can actually be observed and modeled. Best of all, there's one in your neighborhood.

The playground.

Many years ago when my kids were young, one of my favorite things to do while my wife was out was to load my three children in the car, grab a cup of Starbucks, and head for this lab on a beautiful Saturday afternoon. I would open the car door, let my children (we'll call them "the subjects") loose, and plop myself down on the park bench to begin my analysis. As I reviewed one of my journal entries from those years, here's a sampling of what I observed: My six-and-a-half year-old, Kyra, headed for the balance beam, walking back and forth at least six times, talking and laughing to herself, not falling once. My four-and-a-half-year-old, Jeremy, hopped on the stationary motorcycle and began chasing imaginary robbers, narrowly avoiding imaginary buildings and roadblocks with ease, making screeching sounds with his voice that rivaled the best Steven Spielberg special effects. And, yes, my twenty-month-old, Camden. Where was Camden? Ah, there he was—lying on his back, burying himself in woodchips, staring up at the sky and pointing at the clouds. Of course, they weren't clouds to him; he was calling out names like "ball," "car," "mommy," and other things that the clouds shape-shifted into (and out of) with ease.

What great memories! Every time I went to the playground with my kids, I saw dozens of other children creating castles in the sandbox, swinging as high as possible as if to reach the sky, climbing backward up the "swirly slide" and hanging on to the merry-go-round as they spun for minutes on end. As I sat there observing, occasionally looking at my watch, I noticed something startling: not one of the children ever seemed to get tired. They would go from one activity to another with endless enthusiasm and abandon. I never heard one child ask their parent what time it was, how long it was until they could leave, or say that they were bored.

They had a fuel that never ran dry.

The fuel that never runs dry, that all of us get as our birthright, is the fuel of *passion*. In my view, contrary to some self-help manuals, a passion for life is not something that we need to con ourselves into through affirmations and endless soul-searching; it is something that is our birthright. We need only to rediscover it. And while your pursuit of the Top 1% may provide an initial sense of energy and passion unlike anything you have ever experienced, without a doubt, at some point, you will reach a "desert" period—where that passion seems like a distant memory, and the daily activities of life leave you bored, exhausted, and parched for sustenance.

For many of us, as the years go by, our lives become complicated by increasing levels of responsibility—financial, professional, personal, and spiritual. How can I provide for my family? Am I saving enough for retirement? Am I really doing what I love? Am I advancing in my career as I should? Why isn't my marriage more fulfilling? How can I spend more time with my spouse, yet give the time to my kids that they need? What is my life all about, anyway? Why am I here? Where is God in all of this?

Think of life as an artichoke. Our childlike passion and zest for life is contained in the heart of the artichoke, but as the years go by, each challenge and question I just described is like a leaf of the artichoke. Each question, each challenge, adds another leaf, and what remains is just a taste of our passion. Rarely do we have the time or the energy to peel it all away to the core.

I don't want to be simplistic by saying that all of us overly sophisticated adults need to just get with it and live as children do. Obviously, the older and more successful we become, the more complex life can, and will, become. Success and leadership requires that we not shy away from these complexities and challenges, but, indeed, embrace them and bear the burden of rising to meet them. To borrow again from one of my favorite authors, Dan Sullivan, I am suggesting that we rise above our ceiling of complexity to reach a new "higher" level of simplicity. We need to turn the wild and wooly world of the marketplace and our personal lives into a "playground" of sorts.

Here are the rules of the "playground" that I've observed. You can apply them to achieve a higher level of simplicity and tap into your fuel reserves:

1. **Be present wherever you are.** Continually discipline your mind and your soul to experience whatever you are doing with full attention. If you can reduce the

distractions in your mind by only 50%, you will be amazed at the additional energy and creativity this will unleash. Check out books and audio programs on meditation, relaxation, and concentration to learn ways of disciplining your mind to stay present.

2. **Live according to your own internal standards.** The older we get, the more we seem to be concerned with what the "Joneses'" do, how they live, what they earn, what they wear, what activities their kids are involved in, and even what they believe. Stephen Covey says it best: "Stop confessing other people's sins." I would add, "Stop living your life according to external cues, and live according to what makes the greatest amount of sense to you." Your fuel reserves can only be tapped if you are turning on the jets—not if others are at the controls. My son Jeremy didn't care if other kids were having more fun on the swirly slide, he was too busy catching robbers and dodging buildings!

3. **Dial up the curiosity factor.** It is easy to get locked into routines as we get older. Get up, eat breakfast, work out (hopefully), get the kids dressed and to school, go to work, race home, eat dinner, catch up with your spouse on the day, give the kids a bath, fall asleep on the couch—then rewind, reset, and rerun. Nothing saps our passion reserves like routine. How do we beat this?

Certainly we can try to vary our routines a bit, but to a certain extent, routine is a necessary part of life and not completely avoidable. The better strategy is to practice the art of curiosity and wonder. Spend some of your early morning time reading about things that you are fascinated with, whether they relate to your career or not. Make a point to put aside your "judging mind" and turn on your "curious mind," whether you are engaged in a conversation or putting together a business presentation. Remember, there's a gold mine in those clouds, if you'll only look a bit more closely.

4. **Finally, laugh.** Make laughter a part of your daily routine. Use it to smooth over life's rough patches, put silly or petty grievances in perspective, and keep your friendships strong. I've come to the conclusion that a person's mental health is directly related to the number of belly laughs they have each week. As the Bible says, "There is a time to laugh and a time to cry." I'm not being simplistic by saying laugh at everything; life isn't just "small stuff." But most of us have given our tear ducts a much better workout than our abs.

Do these things on a regular basis and you'll burn that precious fuel that never runs dry—the fuel of passion.

# 19

# The Gift That Lingers

It has probably been repeated one too many times that we live in the information age. We hear it so often that we likely take it for granted. "Well, of course," we think, as the latest economist waxes poetic about our need to become "knowledge workers," as if the workers of the bygone era were nothing but mindless automatons. Indeed, "information age," "new millennium," "age of the machines," "virtual reality"—the catchphrases of the last ten years—have reached the point where we can now call them trite.

Tired as they may be, we cannot deny their truth. Indeed, the fact that we cannot shake them is evidence of their truth. We are awash in information in every area of our lives. Thousands of brand-new e-books are launched every year. The 100 e-mail day is typical for the average executive, and productivity expert David Allen tells us that the 200 e-mail day is not far behind. The Internet access right on our smartphone can bring us instant information on any product we want to buy, politician we want to vote for, city where we want to live, or person we want to date. Yes, we have plenty of information, and that's a good thing. Or is it? Believing that all truth is ultimately paradoxical, I'm going out on a limb to say, "Yes and no." Yes, certainly, more information has made our lives richer in a myriad of ways. With better information, we can make better choices about the products we buy, the cities we live in, the schools our children attend, the medicine we use, and the job we take. And yes, more information widely dispersed is a virtue in a democratic society that values freedom and abhors centralized control.

But I am going to argue just as strongly that, in many ways, more information has made us poorer—poorer in wisdom. And I have the strong suspicion that you, too, have been feeling this for some time. Yes, I get 100 (often poorly written) e-mails a day, but rarely if ever do I get the heartfelt, well-constructed letter. Yes, I do have more information on that political candidate, but depending on what website I'm reading, it can be so fraught with ad hominem attacks, unsubstantiated rumors, and poorly constructed reasoning that I can hardly trust the source. After all, what qualifications does someone need to post information on a website? And of the hundreds of books I've read over the last three years, I would count twelve of them as having enough wisdom to justify a permanent place on my physical or virtual bookshelf. Most of them repeat what scores of other books have said, with a new title and a heavy dose of PR to convince us of their validity. Yes, I must admit, these days I have more information than ever, but I have to dig deeper than ever for wisdom. And if you are serious about distinguishing yourself, not only as a successful member of the Top 1%, but as a fully actualized and well-rounded human being, you must continually mine the information deluge for true wisdom.

What do I mean by *wisdom*? In many ways, it is difficult to define. It's hard to define love, but I know it when I feel it. It's hard to define beauty, but I know it when I see it. And it's hard to define wisdom, but I know it when I hear it or experience it.

One of the best ways I can think of to describe the difference between information and wisdom is in thinking about your dreams. I can't tell you how many times I have had a powerful, vivid dream that wakes me up in the middle of a deep sleep. Then, as I turn to my wife to tell her about it, it slips from my mind, literally as I'm describing it to her! A few minutes later, it's completely gone, and I'm back asleep. Experts tell us that we dream dozens of times every night, some that we remember briefly, but most that we will never recall. Yet, I have some dreams from my childhood that were so powerful that I can still remember them to this day in great detail. In fact, they made such an impact that when I describe them I suddenly feel myself thrust back into the consciousness of my childhood. Therein lies the difference. Wisdom lingers; information dissipates. Wisdom is the smell of the rose that registers in the heart; information is the whiff of a burning candle as it is swiftly blown out.

I like to break down wisdom into two categories: *unconscious* wisdom and *conscious* wisdom. Unconscious wisdom arises out of innocence. It is an action, thought, or statement that occurs without reflection; it is pure, simple, and often young or new. Conscious wisdom arises out of maturity. It is an action, thought, or statement that occurs with great reflection or consideration; it has many facets or complexities in its origin, is simple in its expression, and is often old or aged. If wisdom were a drink, unconscious wisdom would be freshly squeezed orange juice; conscious wisdom would be a fine wine.

Probably the best way for me to illustrate the difference between the two is to give you an example of each from my own life. Fortunately, both of these examples have something in common. I call the theme of these examples "one more french fry." Often the best source of unconscious wisdom is, of course, children. By definition, they are innocent and pure, and their actions, thoughts, and statements are often impulsive. These are the very qualities that make those unplanned moments with your children all that more special. My three teenage children continue to be founts of wisdom for me, but as those of you who are parents of teenagers probably know, it's difficult to get teenagers to communicate that wisdom with you (they save it for their friends on social media!). It's those younger years that really stand out, not only because one's children are so uninhibited at that age, but because their childlike simplicity makes their wisdom stand out in a way a parent never forgets.

On one occasion, about twelve years ago, I had the unique opportunity to spend three entire days alone with my children. My wife, Elvia, had taken a well-deserved break to go and visit an old college friend for the weekend, and good ole dad was left to hold down the fort. The first two days we had more fun than we had ever had—playing games, going to the park, making crafts—and I remember the kids even went to bed on time! The third day, the fort came off its hinges. I think I saw a full moon late the night before, but whatever it was, the kids had gone absolutely stir-crazy. The downstairs resembled a war zone—with papers strewn about the living room, marker doodling from our two-year-old on every object *but* paper, and piles of folded clothes disassembled and connected together to make a "tent." Then there was the butter fight. I'll leave that one to your imagination.

Anyhow, given the fact that Mommy was coming home in two hours, I thought it best that we break the routine, and save the house, by going out to dinner. The bewitching hour continued all the way to the restaurant—with the kids tickling, teasing, taunting, and pulling hair—all from their car seats. We got to the restaurant and sat down, I looked as if I had walked through a car wash and felt as if I had aged ten years. I was so frustrated at that point that I could barely talk to the kids. But then, after serving my three children their dinners, the waitress said it would be a few minutes more before mine arrived. Even though I told all three kids to eat, I watched as they all sat and stared at me longingly, refusing to eat before I got my dinner. Then my son Jeremy said, "Dad, I feel bad you don't have something to eat too. You want one of my french fries?"

"Sure, Jeremy," I said. "Thank you. That's very thoughtful."

At that point, our seven-year-old Kyra followed, saying, "Dad, do you want one of my french fries?"

And then followed our two-year-old, Camden. "Daddy, want a *fresh* [as he called it] fry?" From then on, they circled around offering me french fries, one by one, until my dinner arrived. I was hit with one of those unexpected moments with my three kids. Their offering of "one more french fry" was an example of unconscious wisdom. They had long let go of the frustrating day we had and were in the moment, hit with a pure and genuine desire to give to someone they loved. In that one moment, they taught me to let go of any grievance I might have, so that I might keep myself open to give unconditionally, from the heart, to those I love.

The goal in our lives, the path to the greatest amount of happiness and fulfillment for ourselves and to having the greatest impact on others, is to reflect on the examples of unconscious wisdom in our lives and make them a *conscious* way of living. Again, conscious wisdom often does come from age. It requires some experience with life, some time to test out the various options that life gives us, and to ultimately arrive at a place where we can make educated choices that really make a difference. In the example I just gave with my children, I truly did make a commitment to let go of petty disturbances more quickly and to practice unconditional giving wherever I can.

I have even made changes in my life in simpler ways. Anyone who knows me knows that I am somewhat of a health fanatic. I rarely eat sweets, running is my favorite hobby, and I can barely hold my daily vitamin supplements in one hand. Yet as I've gotten older I have found it easier to move from being a health *fanatic* to being health *conscious*. Yes, I can see that health is important. Without health, you have nothing. Yet at the same time, I was letting it get in the way of experiencing my life to the fullest. After all, I told myself, what good is living a long time if you don't get to enjoy some of life's little indulgences? So if you were to spy on me at lunch sometime over the next week, you might see me ordering a plate of french fries with my sandwich and enjoying every one of them. The wise position I've come to is that extremes of any kind are unhealthy. I'm working on radical moderation.

Keep in mind that it is the consciously wise among us who have not only changed their lives, but have changed civilization. If Gandhi had listened to all of the experts and gathered all of the available information on how to fight a war, rather than consulting the wisdom of his own heart, he never would have brought Britain to its knees without firing a single shot. Wisdom isn't often found in conventional thinking. It contains both unconventional and conventional ideas. Conventional thinking says, "Just go do it," or "Take action." Conscious wisdom says for some situations it's best to tell someone, "'Don't just sit there, do something," and in other situations, "Don't just do something, sit there." Conscious wisdom can't be stereotyped. It is unpredictable. But conscious wisdom is how heroes are born. Conscious wisdom changes civilizations. Conscious wisdom stays with your children long after you're gone.

Conscious wisdom stays with the student, long after the mathematical theorems are forgotten.

So take some time over the next few weeks to sift through all of the information that you have learned in your life. Determine which ideas you need to keep, change, adapt, or discard. Then take that gift of wisdom and wrap it up in your own unique package. Give this gift often to others—especially your loved ones. It's the only gift that lingers.

# 20

# The Grand Conspiracy

HOW THE TOP 1% FIND PURPOSE
AND FULFILLMENT

Several years ago, a friend gave me a book by A. Ralph Epperson called *The Unseen Hand*. The subtitle, almost as provocative, was *A Conspiratorial View of History*. The book contained scores of imaginative—some would say ridiculous—theories about how the whole of history was controlled by a very small group of individual families, with a singular, cohesive goal of mind control and world domination. The Federal Reserve hoax, black helicopters monitoring the public, and contrived world wars with pre-planned outcomes were just a few of the ideas that were offered. After I reflected on my own personal experience of the often chaotic and unplanned nature of events in our human lives, I tossed out almost all of the large-scale conspiracy theories—and concluded that they were mostly a good form of entertainment—and, of course, a good source of book royalties.

While I threw away many of the accusations as implausible and far-fetched, I must admit that the book's theories were difficult to dislodge from my consciousness. And I did preserve my belief in one large-scale conspiracy theory. Ironically, it's one that was left out of that provocative book. It is the worldwide conspiracy to keep each and every one of us from living an extraordinary life.

To begin, I need to define terms. By *extraordinary*, I mean a life of deep and lasting fulfillment, purpose, and joy. I mean a life in which one has few regrets and a collection of unforgettable moments upon which to reflect.

Now, you might ask, who is behind this conspiracy? And how are they keeping us from living an extraordinary life? In many ways, every one of us is behind the conspiracy. It comes from our desire to construct our lives from what I call a "bottom to top" philosophy. We all want to get to the top. In fact, that's one of the goals of this book—to get you into the Top 1%. In many ways, the whole idea of the top is the metaphor of the American Dream. When we leave school and enter the workforce, we are trained—by the media, merchants, advertisers, and truth be told, many personal development experts and gurus—to pursue the "three gets": (1) get rich; (2) get noticed; (3) get influence.

We fall prey to the major tool of the conspiracy: *measurement*. After all, the only way you can determine if you've gotten to the top is to measure whether you've reached the highest pinnacle of the success mountain. Money is something you can measure. Simply count the amount of money you have, and you can measure how close to the top of the mountain you are. You can also measure how well-known you are by counting the number of entries for your name in Google, the number of your connections on LinkedIn, the number of articles written about you in major publications, and the number of people who are vying for your time. You can count how influential you are by totaling the number of people who report to you or work for you, the number of people who subscribe to your newsletter, or the number of "successful" people you count as friends.

But as you'll soon see, there are many problems with a bottom to top philosophy, where success is subject *purely* to measurement. First, anything that cannot be easily measured is ignored. As a result, many of the most precious moments in life—those not easily tallied as key stepping-stones to success—cannot be appreciated. Second, life is always a pursuit to *get* somewhere—namely up to the top—rather than to *be* somewhere—namely where you are now, in this present moment, the only moment that exists. Third, all of the "gets" are lies. They do not lead to an extraordinary life. An impressive study by financial expert Jean Chatzky, outlined in her book *The Ten Commandments of Financial Happiness,* reinforced earlier studies of wealth and happiness. Her conclusions showed that happiness and fulfillment do increase for someone moving from poverty to a middle-class existence. But beyond a surprisingly low level of income (approximately $50,000), there is *no measurable increase* in happiness or fulfillment.

Getting noticed doesn't fare any better in the fulfillment department. There is always someone who is better known, always someone whose star is rising faster. In fact, as my friend Harvey Mackay, author of numerous business books, including *Swim with the Sharks without Being Eaten Alive,* always says, "Never try to catch up with the Joneses. As soon as you do catch up, they refinance." Relying on popularity for fulfillment is like betting your extraordinary life on the craps table at Vegas: some days you're up and some days you're down, but the cards are stacked against you. This is not to say that wealth and recognition are not important. Indeed, in their proper context they are vitally important. But, truth be told, getting rich and getting noticed are by-products of extraordinary living. To seek them directly, with a fervent, if not obsessive, focus is too likely to lead one to an unbalanced life where even money and applause will not satisfy. That's why this book has focused on the whole of successful living—not just reaching the Top 1% in terms of income, but being a special subset of that group that wants to live in an extraordinary way—in every important area of life.

If getting rich and getting noticed doesn't lead to an extraordinary life, where does an extraordinary life come from, and how can you assure that your life will be truly fulfilling, purposeful, and joyful?

The first step is to reorient your life philosophy from a "bottom to top" approach to what I call a "timeline" approach. With this approach, rather than building a life from bottom to top, you work from the end back. At the very left-hand side of the timeline is your current life state—your current age, the current state of your family life, your occupation, your dreams, your desires, your anxieties, hopes, and fears—in short, your life as you know it now. All of this exists at the far left end of the timeline. Then, at the far right end of the timeline is the day before your death. You might imagine what age you are, where you live, how you feel, and what your dreams, desires, anxieties, hopes, and fears will be at that point in your life.

Now comes the most important part of all. Sit down in a quiet place, close your eyes and try to imagine yourself at that time in your life, sitting at the kitchen table in your home with a cup of coffee and enough time to think about the life you have lived. Imagine, as best you can, that you are reflecting back on the most rewarding, fulfilling, and joyful times in your life—those things that have made life truly worthwhile. And, if you can, imagine any regrets that you might have—especially if you continued to live your life on your current path.

After doing this exercise for about fifteen minutes, open your eyes, get a pen and a piece of paper, and write down the lessons that you have learned. After you have done this, compare these lessons with the reality of your current life state. Reflect on how you might reorient your life to be more consistent with the most rewarding, fulfilling, and joyful aspects of your life one day before your death. Even more, reflect on how you might eliminate those activities, habit patterns, and beliefs that led to the greatest regrets you had in your older age.

I've found that this strategy is a far more powerful goal-setting strategy than any others I've ever considered, because it begins at the place where our lives will be evaluated: at the very end of our journey. It nearly ensures that our life will be deemed extraordinary.

But for those of you who had trouble visualizing just how you might feel about your life many years from now, I'd like to supply you with a new list of "gets" that my research has revealed about people who have the luxury of reflecting on their lives before they leave their earthly existence. These three "gets" provide a road map to an extraordinary life.

1. **Get connected.** Study after study shows that over 80% of our happiness comes from our relationships with other people—and most specifically, the six closest relationships in our life. Yet very few of us—especially men—have ever read a book on how to establish closer, more fulfilling relationships. Don't leave it to chance. Make your connections to others, and to God, your top priority in life. If you're looking for a single guideline to get you on the right track, remember Earl Nightingale's maxim: "Our rewards in life will always match our service." Make service to others your aim, and not only will you have enough close relationships to share the joys, trials, and tribulations of life, but you'll also have more wealth—tangible and intangible—than you ever dreamed of. Service to others is not only great for building personal relationships, it's good business.

2. **Get real.** Tom Peters, one of the greatest authors and thinkers on business success, made one of his classic witty yet insightful comments when he said at a speaking event, and I paraphrase: "The blessing of being in your mid-sixties is that when you speak, you no longer care about being invited back."

His point was that the blessing of age was the freedom it gives you to say what you mean and act how you truly feel, without much concern about what others think. What a lesson this is for you and me, and our path to an extraordinary life! Where would you live, whom would you spend time with, what occupation would you have, what political party—if any—would you belong to, what beliefs would you hold, if you truly put aside what others thought and went with your own instincts? Think about this hard, at a very deep level. If we're truly honest with ourselves, there are probably one or two areas of our lives that need to "get real."

3. **Get passionate.** The only thing we will spend our time on, especially the day before our death, is that which we are most passionate about. I know for me, I'll have a cup of gourmet coffee in hand, the Notre Dame Victory March playing in the background, my bookshelf of nonfiction classics and audio programs behind me, my God above looking down at me, and my wife and three precious children at my side. All the things I spend time on now because they are what I ought to do, or am expected to do, will be long gone. We can't totally eliminate all the mundane activities of life, but we can make a commitment to spend the majority of our time with the people and on the things that truly matter.

The best news of all is that living by these three "gets" actually nets you five! It nearly assures that the by-products of getting rich and getting noticed will be yours on your road to the Top 1%.

The truth is that the timeline exercise is not just a fun technique for young people to reflect on their old age. For some people on our planet, even very young people, today is the day before their death. None of us have a guarantee on the number of days we'll live. Let this reality liberate you to lift the veil of the Grand Conspiracy. Get connected, get real, get passionate—and live an extraordinary life!

# 21

# Five Reasons to Be Optimistic about Your Future

WHY THE TOP 1% ARE DYNAMISTS

By investing your time and resources in this book, you have already demonstrated a deep faith in yourself. You are willing to invest in yourself for the ultimate long-term benefit of greater growth, success, wealth, and most importantly, fulfillment. Yet on this journey of self-discovery, you are going to have to overcome a persistent cultural fear that seems to be growing in severity—namely the fear of the future. Whether it's by our major media outlets, new book releases, or political discourse, more often than not the future is not discussed in glowing terms. Radio and television networks, book publishers, and even our politicians know that "doom and gloom" sells. Why is this?

There are two major reasons—one personal and the other sociological. On a personal level, most people are afraid of change and find it much easier to remain in a comfort zone of their own making. Doom and gloom sells because it reinforces our belief that taking risks is foolish, that innovation is risky, and that we are much better off protecting and preserving our status and position.

On a sociological level, the actual pace of change has so dramatically increased over the past ten years that we are facing the reality of exponential levels of growth in nearly every area of our lives—levels of growth unprecedented in the history of mankind. It is said that more changes occur now within five years than occurred within fifty years for our grandparents' generation. Such astounding changes are difficult to forecast—and can thus produce a sense of anxiety about what the future will be like. And since the unknown is always a bit scary, we see movies like *The Matrix, Minority Report,* and more recently, *Ex Machina,* which forecast a world in which technology struggles for superiority over man.

However, we intuitively know that in order to grow as human beings and to passionately pursue our goals, we must approach the future with confidence and enthusiasm. The distant goal of success, in any endeavor, cannot be reached by running around in circles within your comfort zone. Like a rocket headed for the moon, to reach your destination, you must break through the pull of gravity, the pull of the comfort zone , to accelerate toward your chosen destination.

Fortunately, you do not have to approach the future with a blind, Pollyannaish optimism. There are five very good reasons to be extremely optimistic about your future and the future of our world.

1. **Despite what the newspaper headlines say, hard research has proven the incredible progress in every major area of life over the past fifty years. Things really are getting better.** You don't believe me? Just listen to these figures. Statistics show that life expectancy is a record high around the world—and growing. The U. S. death rate from heart diseases has dropped 40% in the last two decades. Despite the sensational headlines, corporate downsizing affects only about 3% of the total U. S. labor force—while the resulting increase in self-employment is a net benefit, with self-employed people earning more than 40% more per hour than people who work for others. Only about a century ago, there were but a handful of democracies on earth; now democracies are flourishing. There are some ten million private businesses in the United States today, four times the number as recently as 1970. And leisure time and the activities that go with it—like spending extra time with family, traveling, reading, et cetera—are dramatically increasing worldwide.

2. **Technology has increased our choices and thus our opportunities for greater success and fulfillment.** The evidence is clear that whether it be the Internet, e-mail, new drugs to eliminate or manage disease, or smartphones, smart homes, and smart cars, increases in technology allow human beings to be more efficient, getting more done in less time, while spending more time focusing on creative, as opposed to routine, tasks. The Internet, in particu-

lar, has dramatically increased our choices for success, by allowing us to work wherever we like, while having instant access to a global marketplace.

3. **Success, to a greater and greater degree, is based on merit—and is therefore completely within your control.** The days of succeeding because of company politics, tenure with a company, gender, race, and other types of smoke and mirrors are nearing their end. The collapse of hierarchies and the retooling of organizations and our economy will not permit companies to survive, especially in a global marketplace, unless they are incredibly productive. This ensures that, more and more, companies will continue to track the value that you add as an individual, disregarding other, non-merit-based factors. This is great news for people like you and me, committed to personal development.

4. **Greater financial control over your future gives you greater ability to focus on what's really important.** Imagine—more than fifty million Americans now own stock in individual companies or shares in stock mutual funds. This is astonishing, especially given the fact that just a generation ago investing was the realm of the upper classes only. In addition, new financing options have dramatically increased home ownership and college savings. The average person, with the financial tools available to him or her, by making the commitment to save just 10% of his or her income starting at working age, can almost certainly accumulate a net worth from

$500,000 to $1 million. This increased financial flexibility gives us the resources to increase our lifestyle, whether that means spending more time with our children, traveling more, or starting a new business.

5. **What has not changed, and will never change, is Earl Nightingale's success secret—we become what we think about.** Regardless of what the future holds, we are in control of our destiny, because we are in control of our thoughts—and with our thoughts we paint our world. Particularly in a knowledge-based economy, nothing will impact the quality of our future more than the quality of our thinking. Our future is in our hands—or, more appropriately, our minds.

One of my favorite books about how to view the future from the perspective of a person who aspires to be part of the Top 1% is a classic titled *The Future and Its Enemies* by Virginia Postrel. In it, she noted the differences between those who embrace the future and those who fight the future. She even gave them names—*dynamists* and *stasists*. Dynamists embrace a world of constant creation, discovery, competition, evolution, and learning. Stasists, on the other hand, embrace a more regulated, engineered world of stability, control, and predictability.

So let me ask you, which type of person has the greatest chance of success? More importantly, which type of person are you? Make the decision to become a dynamist. Review the five reasons above and embrace your future. Remember, like it or not, the future arrives for everyone.

# 22

## Choices vs. Priorities

Recently, on the way back from a trip to visit some extended family about forty-five minutes from our home, my wife nonchalantly asked me to pull into Walmart so she could pick up a "few things." If you're like me, you've fallen for this trap. Your spouse mentions that they'll just be a minute or two so they can pick up a gallon of milk and some batteries, and then forty-five minutes later, you've nearly died from carbon monoxide poisoning in the car, the kids have already reached the REM sleep stage, and your spouse comes out with six bags of everything from wheat germ to Cheez Doodles. And, darn! They forgot the batteries!

Nope, I wasn't going to fall for that trap this time. As I pulled into the Walmart parking lot, I saw the row of cars idling in front—I've nicknamed it Death Row—

with scores of other people who fell for the "be just a few minutes" game.

"That's all right, honey," I said. "I'll go in and get the few things this time."

I pride myself on being a "laser beam" shopper. By that, I mean a shopper who catapults into the store, focuses on the one or two things (and *only* the one or two things) on the list like a laser beam, and then checks out as soon as possible.

"That's fine," my wife, Elvia, said. "We only need some toothpaste for the kids anyway. And I'd rather not fight the crowds."

So I ran in. When I got to the toothpaste aisle, I nearly collapsed from paralysis. All I wanted was toothpaste—and here were my choices: whitening with peroxide, whitening with tartar protection, gel, paste, combination gel and paste, berry flavored, mint flavored, Colgate, Crest, Aquafresh, squeeze tube, no-spill pump-style tube, gingivitis protection, bad breath protection—need I go on? I stood in the aisle, picking up tubes and putting them down, reading labels, comparing unit prices, weighing the taste factor against the whitening factor—aaahhh! It was all too exhausting. So I emerged from the store over thirty minutes later with several different tubes of toothpaste (not to mention milk and orange juice!), and handed them to my wife—who was grinning from ear to ear.

Choices. We live in a world of unprecedented choices. The magnificent global economy in which we live and work in the twenty-first century provides more choices for us over a five-year period than our grandparents experienced in their entire lifetimes. And if the economy keeps up this pace, our children will experience the same level of choices in a month or less.

A certain level of choice is a good thing. Choice provides freedom—it allows us to control the direction of our lives to a greater degree, and to customize nearly every life experience to our liking. It is the era of the double shot decaf latte with a shot of hazelnut, a night of customized entertainment on Netflix, and Siri to tell us the best new book to read based on our "preferences." But is more choice, ad infinitum, necessarily a good thing? Or is it possible that too much choice can actually be restrictive, unnecessarily complicate our lives, and lead to greater unhappiness?

This might sound counterintuitive, but it is the conclusion reached by perhaps the most profound book that I have read over the past decade. It is called *The Paradox of Choice: Why More Is Less* by Barry Schwartz. If you haven't read it, I recommend that you pick up or download a copy for yourself as soon as possible. Not only is it a great read, but it will stretch your mind to a new dimension of understanding about what is important in life, what truly makes you happy, and how to make some important, yet perhaps countercultural decisions about limiting the number of choices you allow in your life. As a person who aspires to be part of the Top 1%, you need to make sure that you make choices wisely and protect your time by refusing to lose yourself in the white noise of endless options. Here are some of Dr. Schwartz's main arguments:

1. We would be better off if we embraced certain voluntary constraints on our freedom of choice, instead of rebelling against them.
2. We would be better off seeking what is "good enough" instead of seeking the best.
3. We would be better off if we lowered our expectations about the results of decisions.
4. We would be better off if the decisions we made were irreversible.
5. We would be better off if we paid less attention to what others around us were doing.

At first glance, this might appear to be a prescription for mediocrity. You might be thinking, "I've been striving to stretch my potential, to fully use all of the talents I've developed, and to achieve great success, and now you're asking me to lower my expectations and settle?"

Not exactly. What Dr. Schwartz suggests, and what I wholeheartedly endorse, is making conscious choices about *when* to choose in our lives. For those areas that we have determined are of the highest importance and greatest value to us, we should, without question, strive to maximize our talents and achieve the highest levels of success possible.

The problem is that our modern culture endorses greater choice in every area of life, regardless of its importance. This is, no doubt, why we often feel overwhelmed and paralyzed by the amount of work we have on our plate. The e-mails and phone mails keep piling up, the projects around the house continue to multiply, there are dozens of choices to make at the supermarket, dozens of options to choose from for vacation, dozens of websites to surf for the best deals. The list goes on and on.

Here is the key distinction: *Come up with a list of your top five priorities in your life right now.* Write them down on a three-by-five index card. After you have done so, commit to putting 80% of your time and focus into these areas and these areas only. The other areas of relatively little importance should receive only 20% of your time, and you should limit your choices in these areas as much as possible.

For example, spending time with my family is a top priority for me. Getting the best tube of toothpaste is way down the list. Rather than wasting thirty minutes looking for the best toothpaste, I should have grabbed the first and best intuitive choice and moved on. That time investment was not worth spending an additional twenty-five minutes away from my family. I could have invested the same amount of time singing a song with my kids in the car.

In what areas of your life do you find yourself wasting an inordinate amount of time on choices that ultimately make very little difference and are not even close to your top five priorities? Make the decision right now to limit your time investment choosing in these unimportant areas. The simplicity and focus it will bring to your life will be amazing.

Here are a few other great ideas from Dr. Barry Schwartz on how to wisely limit certain choices in your life:

1. **Satisfice more and maximize less.** Barry Schwartz uses the term *satisficers* to apply to people who be-

lieve that a "good enough" choice is good enough. They do not have the need to endlessly survey the limitless choices available to be absolutely 100% sure they have gotten the best deal, have asked the best available person for a date, have chosen the absolutely best job, et cetera. Maximizers, on the other hand, do fall prey to needing to maximize every choice available. Especially in those areas that do not fall into your top priorities, choose to satisfice more, and thus radically simplify your life.

2. **Think about the opportunity costs of opportunity costs.** Looking at every choice as a potential opportunity cost is a great exercise for financial planners and accountants in their professions, but it is a lousy way to manage your entire life—especially your personal life. It's hard to justify taking an afternoon to read a book on a hammock or play catch with your son, but sometimes those things that nourish the soul cannot be quantified. Most often, you're best off going with what you intuitively feel your son or your own soul needs and forgetting how financially rewarding it is.

3. **Make your decisions irreversible.** Most people look at decisions and commitments like marriage, parenthood, belonging to a religious denomination, et cetera, as restrictive—limiting one's freedom. Since most of us think that more freedom is always better, any commitment that can't be changed is likely to be avoided. But the reality is that total commitments, those that are irreversible in nature (or which cannot

be reversed without extreme pain and effort) can be just as freeing as reversible decisions. It is very freeing to say, "I am marrying this person and plan to spend the rest of my life with him or her. It is settled. It is finished." This opens you up to an entirely new level of freedom, within that decision, to learn and grow. And it frees you from having to survey options endlessly without ever laying down roots.

4. **Anticipate adaptation.** In short, every decision you make or success you achieve—buying a new car or house, getting married, getting a raise—you will adapt to over time. It will become "normal." The good news is that it is equally true for your failures or tragedies—as rough as they are, you will adapt to circumstances over time. Barry Schwartz found that, over the long run, both severely handicapped people and completely healthy people ended up being about equally happy over time. Anticipate adaptation, and you'll resist the letdown that causes you to add more complexity to your life to keep you high.

5. **Practice an "attitude of gratitude."** Make the decision to be grateful for everything you do have. And only one form of comparison is allowed—those people who are worse off than you and those circumstances that are worse than yours. But to whom do most people compare themselves? Those who they feel are better off, even though it may be in only one area of life—and one that may not even be that important to them. This is a prescription for

never-ending misery. Keep your gratitude bank full at all times.

Start practicing these ideas tomorrow and see what an incredible difference they will make in keeping your life simple and fulfilling. And you don't need to make this another new program or project to add to your list. You can start with something as simple as a tube of toothpaste!

# 23

## Moment Management

The modern philosopher and historian Richard Sennett has written about the necessity for human beings to create narratives out of their lives. In other words, in order to give meaning to our existence, we must feel that the culmination of our days on earth string together seemingly chaotic events to form a story—a very personal story that only we can tell. A story that is complex, yet genuine. But, most of all, a story with structure, with a clear plot, filled with layers of meaning that, like a great classic novel, reveal new and hidden meanings with every reading.

I'm one of those people who absolutely love to encourage family, friends, and even acquaintances to tell their stories. True to form, some tell a story of heroic adventure, others tell a tragedy, and still others, a work in progress. Yet one of the patterns I notice again and again is the tendency for people to focus on several key moments as turning points in the plot of their lives. They tell of the child that finally made the baseball team after years of struggle to fit in. They tell of the deal that they closed, or the deal that fell through. They tell of the moment that they first realized their partner moved from being a boyfriend or girlfriend into that exceptional "true love" that comes only once in a lifetime. They tell of the day they heard they had cancer, the day that their firstborn emerged from the womb, and the day they buried their mother right next to their father. They also speak of relatively simple things, like cuddling with the kids on the deck as they watch the stars, sipping hot cocoa with their spouse at the top of Pikes Peak, or the first time they walked into their new office after the big promotion. Such moments are precious, and without them our stories would be incomplete. They form the essence of who we are and will continue to shape who we will become.

In our fast-paced world, there is probably no skill that receives more lip service than time management. Indeed, it is a critical skill for success, without which very few people achieve any substantial goal. Yet I fear that too often we have become so focused on the time management essentials—being efficient, opportunity costs, delegation, prioritization, day planners, and iPads—that we end up managing the moments right out of our lives.

This is the nuanced area of time management that few experts consider. We can plan an agenda for a brainstorming session and keep a close eye on the clock, but we can't plan for a breakthrough idea. We can budget in an evening to take our child to a ball game, but we can't budget in the moment in which our child will ask that question about God—one that we have never even considered. We can clear out all the e-mails in our in-box and respond to them efficiently, but we must be careful not to clear out the e-mail with the huge business opportunity, sandwiched between two pieces of spam.

In fact I'd like to try an experiment with you right now. Think back on the last thirty days of your own life. I want you to recount the five most vivid and significant memories that occurred in those last thirty days. Don't strain to remember them—just note the first five memories that bubble up to your consciousness. Pause your reading for a minute and do this now.

Now that you have your five memories in mind, I want to ask you a few key questions. How many of those five memories were events that you planned for—by setting a goal, setting a specific agenda, et cetera? How many of the events occurred spontaneously, with little planning or forethought? Were you surprised how many of them occurred without pre-planning or forethought?

Memories and events that occur with our families are often more spontaneous. Few of us are as structured in our family lives as in our work lives. But such spontaneous events also occur in our work lives far more than we realize. For example, let's say you call a meeting with one of your key partners to plan a new product line for the following calendar year. You set the agenda for the meeting for three hours, with the intention of planning out two new product offerings. An example of a preplanned result would be if the meeting resulted in two great new product offerings.

An example of a spontaneous event would be if the meeting took on a completely new direction, questioning the overall goal of the partnership, and eventually deciding not to just crank out two more products, but to expand the reach of the existing product line through licensing in foreign markets. Neither outcome is right or wrong, good or bad. The difference is that one ended up with the exact result you planned, the other could not have been anticipated.

It might seem as if I'm making the case to pitch your day planner, take a course on Zen, and to blindly run through the valley of chaos and just see where life takes you. But I am much more practical than that. There is no question that creating an organization and structure for our lives through time management and goal-setting is crucial for success. Indeed, as Peter Drucker said in his classic *The Effective Executive,* it is crucial not only to get things done, but to get the *right* things done. And learning the skills of time management is a great way to help us to achieve this goal. But my advice on the *application* of all of these skills is to follow the advice of a popular '80s tune by .38 Special called "Hold On Loosely." Rather than using time management skills to create a rigid structure for your life, where the structure often ends up becoming the idol, use these skills to create a malleable structure that adapts to a given situation.

Think of the rigid structure as a box-shaped room encased with cement on every side. New ideas and experiences can only take the form of the structure, and no new ideas or experiences can penetrate it from the outside: the structure is predetermined and certain. Think of the malleable structure as a large bubble—the kind your children blow into the wind with a wand at a birthday party. The ideas and experiences created within it can stretch it sideways, vertically, and every which way to fit the situation. And occasionally, a great idea or experience can emerge from the outside and pop the whole structure.

There are as many "bubble structures" as there are people. So give this idea some thought, and experiment with new, flexible ways you can apply the skills of time management without managing out those precious moments. This is one of those key distinctions that those of us who wish to live an exceptional Top 1% type of life must make.

Remember that when we come to the end of life's journey, we will look back, much like that experiment I did with you earlier, and recall a kaleidoscope of memories. In many ways, this kaleidoscope will determine the richness and overall satisfaction of our lives. This is why it is so essential to form an "account" of these memories—an account that, just like an investment account, will benefit from compound interest with every passing year. Then, when we reach the age where we are looking back on our lives with even greater frequency, as my grandmother who lived a full life of ninety-eight years often did, we will have a bounty of moments upon which to draw. And as I think back to the smile on my grandmother's face as she would tell me stories about all of her life experiences, I can confidently make you this guarantee: in life's final chapter, the size of your investment account will pale in significance to the size of your "moment account." So start today, and begin making the deposits that will last a lifetime.

# 24

# Real or Popular?

Several years ago I read an interesting article in *The New Yorker* about a man who was then one of the most unpopular people in New York City—Mayor Michael Bloomberg. The article pointed out one of the paradoxes of politics, and it could be said, life in general. The paradox is this: *achievements, quite often, have very little to do with popularity.*

The article went on to describe a list of achievements that, no matter your political persuasion, are undeniable. The article stated that "between the World Trade Center attack and the collapse of the stock market, Bloomberg took office, on New Year's Day, 2002, at something very close to the worst possible moment. Before he had moved—or, rather, not moved—into Gracie Mansion, the city was already facing a budget gap of nearly five billion dollars. Nine months later, the gap had grown to six and a half billion dollars and was on the same scale as the deficit that brought the city to the edge of bankruptcy in 1975."

According to the article, true to Bloomberg's no-nonsense, can-do spirit, he took over the job of mayor like a CEO conducting a major turnaround. This included making some very unpopular decisions. He borrowed two and a half billion dollars. He cut spending by three billion dollars. He raised taxes by three billion dollars. He even doubled fines on parking tickets. The result? The city ended its fiscal year 2004 with a significant surplus, and two bond-rating agencies changed their outlook on the city's finances from "negative" to "stable."

While many of these decisions were painful at the time, Bloomberg's decisions drew praise from politicians on both sides of the aisle. Today it's hard to imagine anyone, in New York or anywhere else across the country, getting bipartisan praise, given our current divided political climate. But at that time, in the mid-2000s, Democrats acknowledged that many of his efforts averted a potential economic disaster in the city. (Bloomberg was a Republican.) Even former Democratic mayor Ed Koch said that "he has done a terrific job and is vastly underappreciated." So why at that time did Mayor Bloomberg's approval ratings hit a low of 24%? That's right: *24%*! According to *The New Yorker,* Mayor Bloomberg's great sin was in not communicating his changes effectively—in essence, not selling them to the public.

One is left with the impression that Mayor Bloomberg was not one for talking about what he would do; he let his actions speak for themselves. It could be said that

Mayor Bloomberg's words understated his passion and commitment to the people of New York. Now that he has finished his time as mayor and has been replaced by Mayor de Blasio, it could be said in hindsight that Mayor Bloomberg, throughout his terms, was always a better doer than a communicator. While I certainly think he could have used a course in sales skills to improve his standing as mayor, I must admit, as I reread that article in light of today's political climate, that I found his understated bias toward action somewhat refreshing.

While I typically stay away from political examples to make a point, I thought that this one had take-home value for all of us across the political spectrum. It highlights one of the major issues of character that any high achiever will confront: *is it more important to be real or popular?* When I have asked this question of other people, they almost always respond: both! And certainly being both real (or put another way, true to yourself) and popular is something that is very possible over the long term. But more often than not, especially in a crisis situation, being true to oneself and to what one thinks is right is not the best way to win a popularity contest in the short term. No doubt Mayor Bloomberg could have looked at the fiscal crisis facing the city and chosen a middle path—say borrowing money and not touching taxes and parking tickets—that would have been much more palatable to the public. But to a man who obviously loves the city of New York and was concerned with more than just winning the next election, he was willing to sacrifice popularity for the sake of the greater good of bringing New York back to prominence.

In the long run, history books tend to be kinder to those who stood by their convictions—especially when the perspective of time can shed light on the positive results that those convictions fostered.

As a high achiever committed to leading your company, your family, your team, or your community, you too will be faced with this decision: *is it more important to be real or to be popular?* And you won't be faced with this decision tomorrow; you'll likely be faced with this decision tonight. Winning popularity contests—be it as a company president, department head, mother, father, or politician—is a loser's proposition. And they are contests that true leaders, members of the Top 1%, don't even enter. While everyone prefers to be liked, the goal of the leader, the person with character, is much more significant than the whim of someone else's preference. The goal of the true leader is to transform the results of an organization over the long term, building a ship that can resist any storm—even storms that she or he will never weather.

True character requires you to make the difficult choice to be real and true to yourself and, quite often, at the expense of your self-interest over the short term. So why go through all of that? Why risk your popularity for some goal that could take years to achieve and that you might not even get credit for? Two reasons: (1) Popularity, like the wind, rises and falls often, independent of our actions. Choose to play the popularity game and you're destined for a life of roller-coaster emotions and a life where you are never settled in your own skin—you're too busy checking out who you must be and what decisions you must make to keep yourself in the game. (2) Being real and making the tough decisions to do what's right casts an approval vote with the one person in the world that makes the biggest difference—you.

So get ready as you leave for work today or attend that community meeting this evening. The decision awaits you. Which will you choose?

# 25

# The Health Asset Account

One area of life that is often overlooked by those who plan to be part of the Top 1% is health. It's easy to convince others that their attitudes, skills, finances, and relationships are important. But, in their passion to work as hard as possible to be successful, they often overlook health, or at least give it a back seat to other priorities. It's not uncommon for successful people to get too little sleep, suffer high levels of stress, and even eat poorly, either because they are eating on the run or eating out all the time when traveling. But the reality is that without good health, you are unlikely to have the energy and stamina it takes, over a long period of time, to be successful. And even if you do reach your goals, what good is it to get to the mountaintop if you are too sick and feeble to enjoy it?

Even for those who are convinced that health is a top priority, deciding what advice to follow on the topic can be very confusing, because in the midst of unprecedented information on it, there seems to be very little wisdom. Numerous health and diet books flood the new release section week by week, with the latest recipe, exercise, or philosophy.

It's what we might call the oxymoron of the "new fundamentals" of health. As personal development author Jim Rohn advised us many years ago, whenever someone says that they have a "new" fundamental, run for the hills. Fundamentals are old and well-established and are not subject to fads or half-formed theories. In this chapter, you can be assured that what you'll hear are the well established fundamentals of getting and staying healthy—based on rock-solid scientific research.

This is a topic that I'm very passionate about because, it's fair to say, outside of my faith and my family, my personal health is my greatest priority. Why? Well, early on in my life I realized it is literally the foundation of everything I would hope to achieve in my life. Every person I wished to influence, every moment I wished to spend with my wife and kids, every career goal I wished to achieve, every destination I hoped to travel to—all depended on my being a healthy, vibrant individual. If I died younger than I needed to, had half the energy that I could have had, or spent most of my life in a sickly state from a disease or ailment that I could have prevented, it would cloud or prevent every achievement that I just listed. And there are millions of people walking the earth today whose moments are half as interesting as they could be, who are influencing a fraction of the people they possibly could, and who have plateaued in their careers or businesses, all because they have half the energy level they were designed to have.

Several years ago I remember getting a new pair of BluBlocker sunglasses. Remember those? They were a mainstay on late night TV infomercials and the source of a lot of jokes. But they were actually a great product. I remember ordering a pair and putting them on for the first time. When I went outside, they were good, but I wasn't overwhelmed by their effect. They seemed no different from any other pair of sunglasses. I was even tempted to return them. Then I noticed a dark film that was affixed to the exterior of the glasses for protection. Once I peeled off the film, put them on again, I was overwhelmed by how much richer and clearer the view was. This was the full BluBlocker experience!

Getting involved in a regular exercise and nutrition program can have exactly the same effect on your life. Your mind operates more efficiently: the film is peeled away. Stress and anxiety melt away, and even the toughest challenges seem manageable. You are more centered, less reactive. You have the energy required for self-restraint under pressure, so you can access a response to a situation that is consistent with your true values. Without that store of energy, your response might have very little to do with your true values. Instead you might give a quick, unprincipled response that merely allows you to blow off steam.

Yes, health, exercise, and nutrition have far more to do with our success in life than we might realize. It is not just a nice thing to fit in if we can into an overloaded schedule. It is *the* key to accessing the best of who we are and to determining who we might become. As my late friend Zig Ziglar used to say, "My schedule is so packed, I don't have time NOT to exercise."

Many successful authors rightly put a huge emphasis on mental attitude as the key to our success in life. Yet many of them mistakenly assume that we can change our attitudes purely as a result of a mental switch we turn on and off in our brains. To my mind, *the* key to maintaining a positive attitude on a consistent basis is participating in a regular exercise and nutrition program. The endorphin rush that you get from a brisk thirty-minute workout and a wholesome breakfast of yogurt and fruit makes a positive frame of mind almost automatic—like a default web page on your computer when accessing the Internet. Rather than having to search for it, it is already there. And the endorphin rush makes it easier to maintain that positive frame of mind all day long. So, in the words of Earl Nightingale, "Attitude is the magic word," but nutrition and exercise are the magic methods for getting there consistently.

Finally, keep in mind that health truly is the highest form of wealth. Many of us spend a great deal of time planning for our retirement financially, but few of us ever plan for how healthy we'll be during retirement. A little thought shows how shortsighted this philosophy is. Can you imagine having a million-dollar net worth at sixty-five, but being too ill to enjoy it?

Sadly, that is the destiny of far too many Americans. The familiar statistic that only 5% of people will ever achieve financial independence could be further cut down if we ask how many of those 5% will be healthy and vital enough at age sixty-five to take full advantage of all the joy that wealth could bring. Traveling with your spouse and children, moving to your dream location, and having enough wealth to live well into your nineties and beyond—none of that will matter if you don't have the asset of your health.

So begin looking at health and longevity as the most important asset account you have. Consider every action you take to improve your health and energy—even if it seems to make little impact in the short term—as an asset that will grow in value for years to come, compounding year upon year, and there to serve you when one of life's precious moments with your family, or in your career, comes your way.

I'd like to end this chapter with four fundamentals for living an energetic, healthy life. Think of each of these four fundamentals as deposits in your health asset account:

1. **Pick a form of exercise that you most enjoy, and do it for thirty minutes, five times per week.** Research shows that just as important as doing exercise is how much you enjoy that exercise. Do something you love, or at least like to some degree, and the benefits you'll receive from that exercise will increase exponentially. For me, my favorite form of exercise is running. But not indoors on a treadmill—I find that laborious and boring. I need to run outdoors, feeling the crisp air and watching the scenery around me, to make it truly enjoyable. And you don't have to be a marathon runner like me. Again, research shows

that thirty minutes of exercise three to five times per week is sufficient to experience positive health benefits.

2. **Eat a healthy, balanced breakfast every day.** Research shows that people who eat breakfast daily are slimmer, healthier, and more energetic than those who do not. So if you're skipping breakfast to lose weight, you're actually doing yourself a disservice. Eating a nutritious breakfast actually speeds up your metabolism. But the key here is *nutritious*. A donut and coffee won't do. It needs to be a balanced breakfast, complete with protein, carbohydrates, fiber, and just a little bit of fat. Yogurt and granola or cereal, with wheat toast and juice is a great choice.

3. **Take a multivitamin supplement every day.** While the jury is still out on taking many herbs and high doses of specific vitamins, most health experts agree that everyone can benefit from a single multivitamin supplement every day. Some recent research also shows that taking supplements in liquid form might be more effective than taking them in pill form— and many such liquid vitamins are now available. However you take it, add a multivitamin to your daily routine.

4. **Practice a meditation or prayer ritual once a day for thirty minutes.** Fascinating studies have been done on Christian and Buddhist monks who have practiced silent prayer and meditation rituals for years and have a biological age of someone fifteen to twenty years younger than their chronological age.

There are several great books and audio programs on this topic, including *Mindfulness Meditation* by Jon Kabat-Zinn, which discuss how to meditate and the benefits the practice can bring.

Add these four deposits daily to your health asset account, and they will deliver dividends of mental and physical wellness that will serve you for a lifetime!

# 26

## The Hero

———————

HOW THE TOP 1% LEAD IN THEIR COMMUNITIES

A few years ago, I read a book from management consultant Dave Arnott that had a great impact on my life, titled *Corporate Cults: The Insidious Lure of the All-Consuming Organization*. The book is a provocative, sometimes alarmist manifesto on how some of the best known corporations listed in the Fortune 500 have begun to take on the same qualities as religious cults. With on-site day care, dry cleaning, and workout facilities, Arnott asserts, most employees would never need to leave the corporate premises—serving the corporations' interests to get as much work out of the employee as possible. Corporate conventions and pep rallies are the equivalent of religious revivals. And, of course, most of these corporations are led by what Arnott calls a *charismatic leader*—making the cult analogy complete.

Perhaps the least provocative but most life-changing idea that Arnott presents in the book is what he calls the *three circles of influence.* In it he has one circle for family, one circle for work, and one circle for community. Arnott says that, in an ideal world, all three circles would be of equal size, because people would give equal time and attention to each. But in actuality, Arnott presents irrefutable evidence that for most people, work is a huge circle, family is a small circle, and community is a tiny, sometimes nonexistent circle. Worse yet, the circles of work and family often intersect, representing the overlap of work into family life—and sometimes vice versa. The model certainly shows the price that family life has had to pay for people's allegiance to work as their primary activity. Even more dramatically, the model shows how civic life in America is, for all practical purposes, dead.

Reflecting on this model, I was saddened, not only for the price that the public arena has paid for our private interests, but also because, by reducing our involvement in our communities, we are missing out on the opportunity to participate in a great concept of leadership. Whether it's your local PTA, American Legion, political action group, church fund-raising committee, or charitable organization, there is a place in your community that is in desperate need of your talents and skills.

In such organizations, leadership is exercised at the grass roots. The top-down model of leadership that most people have experienced in their organizations (which is quickly faltering) is almost always flipped at the community level. Indeed, community organizations and associations are so often in desperate need of your skills that they can put you right where the action is—garnering support for a new computer lab at your kids' school, leading a group of volunteers to a soup kitchen in your town, or taking a group of concerned citizens to Washington for a chat with your congressperson.

What's more, community organizations do not depend on charismatic people at the top, as Arnott describes in corporations. Because the action happens at the grass roots, leaders in your community are much more likely to fit the description of a servant—a person who is great at organizing people, setting a goal or vision, and getting the resources to the people who will be doing the work. Finally, because most people who work in the community are volunteers, the foundation of the work is not necessity, but passion. The maxim is: "I don't have to be here, I want to be here. What can I do to help?" While every human organization certainly will contain the familiar human qualities of competition, politics, and red tape, the fact that one is there for a higher purpose than getting paid seems to help people to rise above such problems a bit easier.

Whenever I hear people cry that there are no heroes anymore, I am certain that they are almost always looking in the wrong place for the wrong thing. They are looking to corporations, the media, celebrities, and sports figures to provide them with heroic leadership. They are looking for a savior who will rescue the masses. And they are continually disappointed. Why? Certainly there are *many* great leaders in *all* of these arenas. But

the myth of the great man or woman on the white horse
that rides in and saves the flock is just that—a myth.
Effective leaders don't depend on charisma and the "wow
or pow" factor (also called the carrot and stick) to make
things happen.

They also don't do it themselves. In a world that is
changing faster in five years than it did in fifty years for
the last generation, no one person can keep up with all
of the factors that are required to lead a team effectively.
We need to jettison this myth of the hero, once and for
all, and replace it with the model of the servant. And the
right place to look for this type of leader is right in your
own backyard—your own community. Make the commitment to get involved in your community and spread
your many gifts and talents around to those who truly
need them.

Then take what you've learned in your community life
and bring the essence of it back to your corporation. Can
you imagine a corporation where the employees didn't
decry the fact that the CEO is asleep at the wheel, but
rather formed their own skunkworks groups to help bring
the corporation into a new market? (*Skunkworks* is name
for a project developed by a small, loosely structured group
of people who are doing radically innovative research and
development. The term originated with Lockheed Martin's
World War II *Skunk Works* project.) Can you imagine an
employee whose daily motivation at the office is not fueled
by the size of his or her biweekly paycheck, but rather by
passion for the product or service?

Yes, in the end, the fact that many people have given up on civic life has hurt them, even more than it has hurt their communities. It has robbed them of the discovery that, when it comes to leadership, they need not waste time looking for heroes; they should spend time *being* heroes.

# 27

# Time is Money, Money is Time

HOW THE TOP 1% WEIGH THE VALUE
OF TIME VERSUS MONEY

In this chapter we're going to be addressing one of the key paradoxes of the twenty-first century. I call it "Time is Money, Money is Time." And this statement is a paradox, because it asserts two seemingly contradictory truths: (1) the fact that we trade time in our culture for the pursuit of money—or better put, for the pursuit of wealth; and (2) the fact that time itself has become a type of currency, a form of wealth—a truth uniquely relevant to our lives in the twenty-first century.

Our lives have become so busy and scheduled, and we are so often interrupted by the ping of texts and e-mails on our smartphones, that free time has become scarce. Thus, as with other commodities in our market economy, the value of time seems to have elevated to an unprecedented level. My goal is to present you with insights from several experts that will help to sort out this paradox and help you construct your own ideal relationship between time and money.

A few months ago, my fourteen-year-old son, Camden, and I took some time out to ride our bikes through a beautiful forest preserve in Antioch, Illinois, where we have lived for many years. I doubt that you've heard of Antioch—even most Chicagoans are not aware of this far northern suburb just a stone's throw from the Wisconsin border. But it is a beautiful suburb—a great place to raise a family, with low crime, a great park district, loads of beautiful green trees dotting the streets, and just minutes from every retail establishment you can imagine. Best of all, housing is extremely affordable. As we rode through the trails of the forest preserve, we came to a bridge that runs over a marsh.

As we rode over the bridge and I looked far in the distance, my memory brought me back to a walk we had taken through Greenwich, Connecticut, some years before, while on vacation visiting family. The scenery was nearly identical. Now I have no doubt that you have heard of Greenwich. It is one of the best-known and most exclusive suburbs on the East Coast—just a short drive from New York City. Greenwich is full of residents who, in terms of income, would fall into the category of the Top 1%. As Camden and I stopped our bikes on the bridge overlooking the marsh, just taking in the gorgeous view, I thought to myself: if I didn't know any better, I would say we were in Greenwich right now, right this very instant.

As I thought about this further, the idea overtook me: was I saying that this forest preserve in Antioch, Illinois, was just as beautiful as the forested areas of Greenwich? I couldn't be saying that. This was Antioch. This was that affordable place, that stepping-stone to an ultimate residential community like Greenwich. But I stayed with the thought—and I came to the conclusion that, ultimately, in this beautiful spot, there was no essential difference between Antioch and Greenwich. The only difference existed in my mind—in how I thought about these two communities, and how those thoughts colored my experience of them.

While it's not my intention to begin discussing this issue with a philosophical treatise, I do think it is important for us to understand how our beliefs and attitudes color our perceptions of time and money, and the fruits of both. It occurred to me, as I reflected on my experience in the forest preserve, that there are millions of people who spend an incredible amount of time and effort to make the money necessary to finally "live the good life" and get to an idyllic suburb like Greenwich. You yourself might be thinking of your goals for the future, where you truly want to live when you've made it, are driving what you truly want to be driving, are wearing what you truly want to be wearing, associating with those you truly want to be associating with, to vacation where you truly want to vacation. While those goals are certainly noble and worthwhile, and while I certainly have nothing against Greenwich or any other exclusive suburb, I believe it is important for us to think deeply about what our pursuit of wealth is truly all about— as Stephen Covey says, "beginning with the end in mind," and to determine whether or not what we need is a shift of lifestyle or a shift of attitude.

I want you to get a mental picture of your life today. Whom you are in a relationship with, where you're working, what position you hold, where you live, what you drive, what you're wearing, where you go for vacation or a little R&R. Hold your present life in your consciousness as best you can for about ten seconds. Focus not only on the picture, but on the feelings. Now let the pictures and feelings fade. Next, insert a new picture. Imagine you are living your ultimate "good life." Get a mental picture of whom you're in a relationship with, where you're working, what position you hold, where you live, what you drive, what you're wearing, where you go for vacation, et cetera. Hold that image in your consciousness as best you can for about ten seconds. Again, focus not only on the picture, but on the feelings. Continue to hold that image.

We're going to try something interesting. I want you to imagine that this good life image has been your known reality for over three years. Feel what it's like to have this reality not as something new and fresh, but something comfortable. You've had your relationship for three years—what does that feel like? What issues do you have? You've worked in your ideal job for three years, and held your ultimate position for three years. What does that feel like? What are your opportunities and your challenges? Continue this process: where you live—your house, your neighbors—what does that feel like now? Next, what you drive—your ultimate car is three years old, you've been driving it for a while, getting comfortable—what does that feel like? Now think of what you're wearing, where you go on vacation. Hold these collective feelings for about ten seconds. Now open your eyes.

What have we accomplished here? With this exercise, I'm trying to give you a little taste (albeit on a surface level) of what psychologists call *adaptation*. Quite often, we unfairly compare our current circumstances—the comfortable circumstances we have lived with for some time, usually three years or longer, to a new, fresh image of a dramatically different life free of challenges, problems, and frustrations. This type of future imagining gives us an ultimately unrealistic picture of what feelings the achievement of our goals would actually create for us. Fascinating studies have been presented by psychologist Barry Schwartz that demonstrate how quickly most people adapt to new circumstances and basically achieve the same level of happiness and contentment that they had previously.

When I did this exercise myself, I found that it was a great tool for determining my true priorities. I could see how a new home would have many of the same things I had currently—just more and bigger. A newer luxury car would get me to and from my location, with a bit more style and comfort, but probably with less reliability and higher maintenance costs. And would that exotic vacation in the Caribbean really deliver me more happiness than a serene trip to a cottage in Door County, Wisconsin? Perhaps, perhaps not, I wondered. What I came to conclude is that the real purpose for wanting to achieve my financial goals as part of the Top 1% was freedom—more free time to spend as I wanted, and with those that I loved.

You may come to different conclusions after you do this exercise. But I do hope it gives you a more realistic idea of what you're trading your precious time for. If you're investing more of your time in the pursuit of more money, to get to the "good life," you might find that you already have the good life—you just need to spend more of your present moments, the time you have now, savoring and enjoying it. And you may find that by avoiding the trap of having to live in an exclusive suburb with the latest model luxury car, given the lessons we learned earlier from the book *The Millionaire Next Door,* will help you to achieve that destination of financial freedom much more quickly.

Building upon my second assertion earlier in this chapter—the assertion that time itself is a form of wealth, how are you investing your currency, your wealth right now, today? You see, I think the "time is money" myth has caused us to turn precious moments into a commodity—a commodity to be traded in the market like a stock or precious metal. When we see time in purely financial terms, every minute that does not service the almighty dollar is a moment wasted.

And yet, again returning to the idea of "beginning with the end in mind," money itself should not be the end. The end is what we think money will give us—the feelings that money will give us. Focus on that end, and you're likely to spend your time not just servicing the almighty dollar, but servicing your true goals. You might also find, to your astonishment, that servicing this end doesn't require any more money at all!

The point here is not that money is bad; it is essential. It educates our children, pays for our homes and cars, funds the charitable organizations that are important to us, pays for the date nights with our spouses, and many other things that we need and enjoy. We need not question money itself. Rather it is the trade-off that we make between time and money that we must question, bring to our awareness, and make sure is in alignment with our true priorities. *Time is too precious to be spent unconsciously.*

Byron Katie, best-selling author of the book *Loving What Is,* has become famous by introducing what she calls the "turnaround." This technique helps people to see the lie of their erroneous belief systems by turning the belief around and seeing if the *reverse* of the belief statement is actually truer than the original belief statement. For example, if I wrote down the belief "I'm frustrated with my spouse because she is so controlling," a turnaround of that belief might be "I'm frustrated with myself because I am so controlling." Katie, as she likes to be known, has produced remarkable transformations in people's lives with this remarkably effective technique. Now if we were to apply the "turnaround" to the belief "time is money," what are we left with? Money is time. Is it possible that the belief "money is time" is truer than the belief "time is money"? Let's test that hypothesis.

There was a remarkable man who dedicated his life to the truth of this hypothesis. His name was Joe Dominguez. He began his career on Wall Street, and through hard work and savvy investing, Joe was able to retire at the young age of thirty. Although he achieved great success, he became disillusioned with the reckless pursuit of the almighty dollar that he saw on Wall Street and began to question the trade-off that millions of people made in their personal and professional lives for the acquisition of money. To him, it seemed like there was no upper limit to this desire. The only objective of the money game was getting more and more, with no end in sight.

Joe began giving seminars called "Transforming Your Relationship with Money and Achieving Financial Independence." The seminar achieved such great acclaim that it was later turned into a book called *Your Money or Your Life,* co-written with Vicki Robin. The book has now become an all-time classic in the financial field. I heartily recommend it. It is unlike any book on finances you will ever read— and it will change your perspective on money forever.

Joe's central assertion, which has transformed so many people's perspective on money, is his *definition* of money. Here is his definition: *Money is something that we trade our life energy for.* To Joe, money is not simply an abstraction, a symbol, or as Tony Robbins says, "a piece of paper with deceased notables" on it. Money is a tradeoff—something that we trade our precious life energy for. And more money, earned or spent, represents a corresponding greater investment of life energy.

With this one statement, Joe turned the tables on the myth that time is money—leading millions into rushed lives, turning every moment into a profit making exercise, in the hopes of acquiring more money to purchase the good life. According to this philosophy, money represents a piece of our life energy—a precious resource that everyone was given a finite amount of at birth, never to be had again.

For millions who understood this philosophy, the question became not "How much can I earn to buy the biggest, the best, and the fastest whatever?" The real question was,

"Is this item worth x amount of my life energy?" For our purposes, the question might be, is my idea of the ideal good life worth perhaps a tenfold investment of my life energy to attain?

Ask yourself that question right now. From the perspective of "money is time," what would your version of the good life be, if you understood Joe Dominguez's critical truth? Are you willing to make the trade-off? For some, the answer will be a resounding "yes"—it's well worth the trade-off. For others, it will be evident that they will need to revise their map of the good life to fit the trade-off that they are willing to make. There is no one correct answer. The only incorrect answer is one arrived at from a place of unconsciousness. Looked at from this new perspective, *money is too important a resource to be spent unconsciously.*

In the end, we see that money and time are really two sides of the same coin, albeit perhaps a different coin than we once thought. Perhaps, like me, you'll reflect on your life and suddenly realize that your lifestyle in the place you live is your Greenwich, your Camelot, and the most important thing is to spend every moment of your life energy appreciating it.

# 28

# Total Availability

I believe that there is a time in everyone's life when the meaning and purpose of existence, and perhaps life in general, crystallizes into a single moment. Quantum physicists use the analogy of the hologram to describe this phenomenon: every part of the holographic image contains all the elements of the entire image. Likewise, how many times have you stopped in the middle of an experience, event, or moment in your life and paused to take a look at it from a larger perspective—reflecting on its total importance while the event is actually occurring?

Movies are the best at capturing these moments and helping us to reflect upon their significance. One of my favorite examples is the ending of *Cheaper by the Dozen,* where Steve Martin is seated around the dinner table at Christmastime, surrounded by his wife and twelve children. As he passes the turkey, the camera focuses on his face as he smiles reflectively and says "yes" to himself— taking in that moment as the essence of all that has come before, the joy of family togetherness.

I had just such a moment in the summer of 2004, a moment that will live in my memory forever. My wife, Elvia, and I, and our three children, who were very young at the time, were in the middle of a two-week road trip across the country in our Honda Odyssey minivan (or should I say, our temporary home?).

We had traveled for two days from Chicago to Virginia Beach, visited with good friends for the weekend, and had just headed out for another two-day adventure (if you have young children, you can imagine what kind of adventure it was!) to visit with my in-laws in West Palm Beach, Florida. At the end of a long eleven-hour driving day, just after 5 p.m. and about thirty minutes from our hotel pit stop in Savannah, Georgia, traffic suddenly came to an abrupt halt. After about an hour of bumper-to-bumper traffic, a truck driver informed us that there had been a huge accident on I-95, one of the major interstates on the East Coast, and that we were ultimately being routed off the expressway to another highway.

As we were all corralled from a four-lane highway onto a single-lane exit, heading for the detour highway, I made special note of a gentleman in a Jeep Grand Cherokee right next to us, who waved us ahead of him as we merged toward the exit. I waved and kept moving forward. As we reached the end of the exit ramp, a policeman directing traffic had just begun waving several cars ahead of us through the intersection. We followed in line across the highway and toward the opposite side of the highway.

Then, in what seemed like an eternity, but was actually a split second, I had the grace to look quickly to my left, whereupon I saw a huge pickup truck heading full speed toward my window. I dove toward my wife, screamed for everyone to hang on, and the truck blasted through my doorway, sending our minivan screeching twenty feet across the highway. In the next few moments, before I could fully register what had occurred, I grabbed the hand of my wife and immediately looked toward the back of our van, where our three children sat stunned, but perfectly secure with their seat belts. My daughter and wife were grabbing me, crying and wondering if I was conscious. I felt nothing physically, but was locked in a zoned-out daze. That's when I looked down and saw the blood down the side of my arm and cheek, with shards of glass embedded in both.

The events that followed were quite amazing. There was the man who pried my door open and began to snap his fingers in front of my face. It was the man from the Jeep Grand Cherokee, the man who graciously let me go ahead, who just happened to be a doctor from a hospital in Gainesville, Florida. He checked me out and took the time to check out my wife and three children and pronounce them in good health before the paramedics arrived. He stayed with us for over an hour. Then there was the man who stopped his car at our side, hugged me and my wife and asked us if we were thirsty. Before I knew it, he was back from the store with five ice-cold water bottles, asking what else he could do for us. Then there was the man from the towing service, who took my wife and kids back to his shop with our car, asked a friend of his to drive me, and spent over two hours with us afterward, counseling us to continue our vacation and giving our kids a tour of his shop while my wife and I tried to regain our bearings. Then there was the staff at the Marriott Courtyard. They found transportation for us back to their hotel after we had searched dozens of transit providers in vain, and then had over four people empty our car as we rested in our room— not to mention the scores of times they checked on us to see how we were recovering. Then there were the scores of phone calls and e-mails I received from family and friends, giving us their support and encouragement, and offering assistance at every turn.

Every time I have been asked about our accident and what it was like, I always respond that while it was shocking, it was one of the greatest blessings my family and I ever received. In that moment, we witnessed a greater demonstration of the power of giving than we had ever imagined. And as I speak these words now many years later, I am more convinced than ever of my purpose for being on this earth: just like the many people who touched me and my family on that fateful day, I am here to give. And, I believe, that you too are here with the same mission: *you are here to give of your talents, abilities, and most importantly, your time.* And the degree to which you are willing to give of these gifts is in direct proportion to the speed in which you will reach the Top 1%. Probably the greatest misconception about reaching the top is the misconception that to do so, you must be a money-hungry narcissist. The reality is that the vast majority of the Top 1% focus their attention on serving others—whether those others are customers, clients, family, friends, or their larger communities. The great Earl Nightingale said it better than I ever could: *"Our rewards in life will always be in exact proportion to our service."*

Yet my image of giving is not the transactional form of giving so popular among many motivational writers today. This form of giving is the one we have so often heard— that of cause and effect. I give to you and do so with the express concern of getting something specific back from you. It is a sanitized form of giving that feigns an interest in another, while truly being part of an overall strategy to move your own goals forward. In this model, you give strategically to those who can help you advance; you don't necessarily give as a way of life—as an expression of your being.

When I look at our accident from a larger perspective, I can see that giving is about more than just you and me. It is part of a grand "divine conspiracy" to move humankind forward. Think of it this way. If I were to give a child a gift or my assistance, you might imagine my hand reaching out to that little child to place something in her hand or to hold her hand and guide her to a given destination. But how is it that God reaches out to us? How is it that God gives us his assistance? Through one another. Each of us, collectively, through our efforts to give our talents, abilities, or time to others, are part of the arm, hand, and fingers of God that reaches out to guide us in our time of difficulty. Yes, we are part of the divine conspiracy.

If this is true, you can see that we need a different model for giving than the transactional model I described earlier. When we are being called to give to another, it may not be at a convenient time for us. There may be no clear way in which we will benefit from our gracious acts toward another. Indeed, in some cases it may, in the short run, cost us financially or even physically. The model I would like to propose is one of *total availability*. I discovered this concept when I was in seminary exploring the idea of the Catholic priesthood, many years ago. As a married father of three, I obviously chose a different path for my life. Yet, without question, the education I received and the disciplined way of life that I practiced while in seminary has been invaluable to me, both professionally and spiritually. And the concept of total availability, while countercultural, was one of the most profound concepts I have ever learned. It taught that we all have a destiny toward which we are called by God. And it is part of our job, through careful discernment and reflection, to determine what that destiny is, and then to become totally available to God and others in pursuing that destiny.

The key idea that made this concept so countercultural was the fact that the destiny toward which we were called may not have been the one that we desired to pursue. Indeed it may have been the least favorite of several options available. Yet, upon careful discernment of our gifts and how those gifts fit with the needs of the community, we were to choose the higher good of serving where the community needed us most. Thus the idea of being totally available, with no restrictions, not even those of our own will. To use the hand analogy again, the transactional model is represented by a tight fist that drops a gift into the hand of another, while the model of total availability is represented by an outstretched arm with an open hand, waiting to assist where it is needed.

This idea might seem contrary to the idea of self determination, but I am convinced it is an idea whose time has come. How tired have we all become of the mantra, preached continually in advertisements, in self-help books and career success manuals, to "look out for number one," or to give your time to the right network of people who can help you advance your career, while disassociating yourself from those who are not on the same fast track.

My friends, such philosophies ultimately lead to a lonely and isolated existence. On that fateful day of our car accident, it would have been easier for the doctor behind us to look with concern and then just drive along. We were not one of his patients, from whom he received any direct benefit. It would have been easier for the local gentleman in his truck not to run to the store and bring back water for people he didn't even know. None of the Marriott staff would have been faulted for not emptying our car late at night and checking up on us regularly—it certainly wasn't part of the official job description. No, fortunately for us, we were touched by the hand of God, the elements of which were several people who made themselves totally available to an out-of-state family from Chicago.

My message is simple: Practice the concept of total availability in your own life. Witness the power of making yourself an open hand to others. Become a member of the divine conspiracy club.

But, you may ask, why should I even bother? What's in it for me? To paraphrase one my favorite authors, M. Scott Peck, if you ask that question, perhaps you don't know enough of joy.

# 29

## Leave a Trail

I am a lover of classic quotations from the great minds of history. In fact, I think everyone would be well served to compile their own treasure chest of meaningful quotes and poems and keep them close at hand, where they can serve you at a particularly challenging or emotional time in your life. One such quote that has served me well is from the American philosopher Ralph Waldo Emerson.

It goes like this: "Do not go where the path may lead, go instead where there is no path and leave a trail." This incredible quote is the perfect way to set the stage for the last chapter of this book. When I reflected on the final message I wanted to leave with you as you embark on your journey to the Top 1%, I realized that there was one quality of character for which every person who aspires to be a successful leader must develop: *courage*. And in many ways, the central message of Emerson's words represents the very essence of courage. The definition of courage that most of us have grown up with is some form of the following: *The willingness to persist and move forward on the path to any worthwhile goal, despite the fear involved.* It's the child who jumps off the diving board for the very first time; it's the junior executive who makes his very first presentation to the board of directors; and it's the mother who takes her first child home from the hospital and begins the journey of parenthood. In its most simple form, these are certainly courageous acts.

Yet the older and more experienced one becomes, the more one comes face-to-face with the other, more complex form of courage. This form of courage requires you to blaze new trails rather than courageously moving forward on existing trails. It is the point in your life where you strive to let your originality shine forth, where you no longer feel that you fit neatly into prepackaged categories, whether it comes to your career, your relationships, your political views, your style of parenting, or your philosophy of life.

I remember some distinct times in my own life where I had such moments of epiphany—where I realized that I was no longer moving down an existing trail. I remember when I no longer felt I could be labeled a Democrat or a Republican, but finally realized that I had a variety of viewpoints from both sides, and proudly announced myself as a "radical moderate." I remember first being troubled by our definition of success in our culture, which too often glorified people who earned big money, while ignoring the champion mother and father who have raised loving and well-adjusted children. I remember going through a crisis in my spiritual life, what some theologians call a "Dark Night of the Soul," where I was forced to reexamine what I truly believed and held dear and to compile a faith that was truly my own.

I have no doubt that you, too, have had such moments. They may or may not be lucid momentary occurrences, but like the leaves from an oak tree in the fall, you may have noticed upon reflection that in some areas of your life you have moved from green to gold.

My suggestion for you, inspired by the great words of Ralph Waldo Emerson, is to muster as much courage as you can to leave a trail in as many areas of your life as possible. Fortunately for me, this book has been my vehicle to communicate a more humane and complex view of success for the aspiring influential leaders in business and in life—the Top 1%—to leave a trail, however small, behind for others. Yet I have a long way to go on this trail, and in many of the other areas I mentioned, my journey has hardly begun.

How about you? What areas of your life have you discovered that your color has changed? In what ways are you unique and different from the conventional paths that have been given to you by your parents, your coworkers, or by society in general? How can you begin to blaze new trails, by "going public" with your uniqueness? For some people, blazing new trails means starting a business that serves a need that the entrepreneur knows is not being served well by any other business. For others, blazing new trails means becoming a community activist to help transform the local education system. For others still, blazing new trails means finally being honest in their relationship with a spouse or dear friend about what they truly believe, who they truly are.

Such acts require immense courage, because not to follow the conventional path is to go against the grain—to stand apart from the crowd. Yet the rewards are more than commensurate with the demands. Because to blaze new trails means to mature into a whole new level of existence, one that exists beyond the continual grasping for happiness to the deeper, richer, and more satisfying experience of joy.

To close, I'd like to pull yet another great quote from my treasure chest. It's a classic poem from Rudyard Kipling, who wrote about such courageous individuals who chose not to follow a conventional road. It was written from a father to his son, but its message is universal and applies equally to men and women.

### If

If you can keep your head when all about you
Are losing theirs and blaming it on you;
If you can trust yourself when all men doubt you,
But make allowance for their doubting too;
If you can wait and not be tired by waiting,
Or, being lied about, don't deal in lies,
Or, being hated, don't give way to hating,
And yet don't look too good, nor talk too wise:
If you can dream—and not make dreams your master;
If you can think—and not make thoughts your aim;

If you can meet with triumph and disaster
And treat those two imposters just the same;
If you can bear to hear the truth you've spoken
Twisted by knaves to make a trap for fools,
Or watch the things you gave your life to, broken,
And stoop and build 'em up with worn-out tools:
If you can make one heap of all your winnings
And risk it on one turn of pitch-and-toss,
And lose, and start again at your beginnings
And never breath a word about your loss;
If you can force your heart and nerve and sinew
To serve your turn long after they are gone,
And so hold on when there is nothing in you
Except the Will which says to them: "Hold on":
If you can talk with crowds and keep your virtue,
Or walk with kings—nor lose the common touch;
If neither foes nor loving friends can hurt you;
If all men count with you, but none too much;
If you can fill the unforgiving minute
With sixty seconds' worth of distance run,
Yours is the Earth and everything that's in it,
And—which is more—you'll be a Man, my son!

And so onward you go, all the way to the Top 1%!

# Index

Printed in the USA
CPSIA information can be obtained
at www.ICGtesting.com
JSHW011536150424
61205JS00015B/696

9 781722 510077